**T E A C H**

CW00503132

WINDOWS 95

Oxford Computer Training

Hodder & Stoughton

A MEMBER OF THE HODDER HEADLINE GROUP

British Library Cataloguing in Publication Data
Oxford Computer Training
Windows 95
I. Title
005.43

ISBN 0 340 63946 6

First published 1996
Impression number   10 9 8 7 6 5 4 3 2
Year   1999 1998 1997 1996

The 'Teach Yourself' name and logo are registered trade marks of Hodder & Stoughton Ltd in the UK.

Copyright © 1996, Oxford Computer Training

All rights reserved. No part of this publication may be reproduced or transmitted in any form or by any means, electronic or mechanical, including photocopy, recording, or any information storage and retrieval system, without permission in writing from the publisher or under licence from the Copyright Licensing Agency Limited. Further details of such licences (for reprographic reproduction) may be obtained from the Copyright Licensing Agency Limited, of 90 Tottenham Court Road, London W1P 9HE.

Typeset by MacDesign, Southampton, Hampshire
Printed in Great Britain for Hodder & Stoughton Educational, a division of Hodder Headline plc, 338 Euston Road, London NW1 3BH by Cox & Wyman Ltd, Reading, Berkshire

CONTENTS

Acknowledgements

A number of products have been referred to in this book, many of which are registered trademarks. These are acknowledged as being the property of their owners.

The trademarks mentioned in this book include:

Microsoft: Windows, Windows 95, MS-DOS, Office 95

IBM: PC

Intel: i486, Pentium

List of Contributors

Jon Collins, Ian Cunningham, Mark Dendy, Ruth Lawrence, Annie Matthewman, Ken Meadley, Peter Othen, Hugh Simpson-Wells, Paul Slater, and the many others from Oxford Computer Group who offered support and guidance during the writing of this book.

1

— INTRODUCTION —

This chapter covers:
- The aims of this book
- The conventions used in this book

This book is intended for users who are new to Windows 95. References to Windows 3.x in the text mean previous versions of Windows, such as Windows for Workgroups 3.11 or Windows 3.1.

This book aims to familiarise users with the Windows 95 interface. It starts with some basic concepts, then goes on to demonstrate many of the powerful features in Windows 95. This book does not directly cover installation of Windows 95. It is assumed that you have Windows 95 already installed on your computer.

This book is not a definitive source of information, and should not be taken to be an authoritative document, merely a guide: an introduction to Windows 95 and a supplement to its manual.

Conventions

Throughout this book, instructions to you are written

like this (in italics, with a mouse graphic to the left).

Anything that you must type is shown `in this style.`

Key words are shown like this: **DOS**, **button**, **Toolbar**, **mouse**.

Special keys are shown like this: Ctrl, T etc. with combinations shown as Ctrl T (press T whilst holding down Ctrl)

On-screen 'buttons' are shown like this: OK

Enter means the enter key (also known as carriage return, return, CR etc.).

References to filenames are shown as `FILENAME.XLS`

Hints and warnings about how to do things are often given in italics like this with a 'thumbs up' symbol at the start.

> *Text appearing in a box with this graphic is usually a technical comment or an aside not strictly essential to the issue under discussion. You may prefer to skip these on the first reading.*

From time to time, you will see a box of summary points which reinforce the section of text that they follow, like this:

> **Summary: Conventions in this book**
> - This book is for users upgrading to Windows 95 from previous Windows versions. It assumes a working knowledge of the Windows interface.
> - Instructions appear in *italics*. Text for you to type appears `in this style`
> - Keywords appear like this: **keyword**
> - This is a summary box, intended to reinforce the points made in the main body of the text.

2

——— STARTING ———
WINDOWS 95

This chapter covers:
- Launching Windows 95
- Logging on

——— Starting Windows 95 ———

A major design goal of Windows 95 is that it should be powerful yet simple to use. This applies to all aspects from installation to shut down.

Windows 95 is an **operating system**; this means that it is loaded and started by your computer (in much the same way as DOS was). Therefore, in many cases, you do not have to do anything other than switch on your computer in order to run Windows 95.

Startup Options

The following section is a little technical. You might like to skip this section on first reading but it contains information on what to do if your computer appears to need user input before Windows 95 starts in full.

Some operating systems allow a concept known as **dual boot**. This means that the computer will pause while stating to allow the user to select the operating system they wish to load. Microsoft Windows NT, for example, can be configured to allow the user to choose between Windows NT and MS-DOS as the operating system to load (although it would be unusual to find this configuration on a stand-alone computer or a simple work-station). Windows 95 can allow the user to boot into the operating system that was installed on their computer prior to the installation of Windows 95. Such systems normally present a simple menu of options, known as a **boot menu** or **Startup menu** and wait for the user to select an option (though some will automatically select a default after a period of time). Full coverage of this subject is beyond the scope of this book; our advice to you, if your computer is configured in this fashion, is to select the option that indicated that Windows 95 will be loaded.

The Windows 95 boot menu has other uses besides allowing a choice of operating systems. In some situations, you may wish to prevent Windows 95 from starting automatically. For example, if you are experiencing problems with hardware such as a network card when using Windows 95, you may wish to load Windows 95 without loading the software used to control the hardware (known as a **driver**). To do this, you can start Windows 95 in **Safe Mode** by selecting the option from the Startup menu. Although Windows 95 can be configured to display this menu automatically, on standard installations, you will find that you need to press symbol F8 when the message 'Starting Windows 95...' appears on screen in order to see the menu. You do not have much time in which to press the key so watch out for the message!

As mentioned above, if you have DOS on your computer as well as Windows 95, one of the options on the Startup Menu will be to load and use DOS instead of Windows 95 as your operating system. An alternative way to make the computer load DOS rather than Windows 95 is to press symbol [F4] when you see the message 'Starting Windows 95...' (although Windows 95 can be configured so as to disable this feature).

In conclusion, today's software is powerful, flexible and adaptable to many situations. Windows 95 contains such a wealth of configuration options that it would be impossible fully to describe each one in this section. However, you should find that it is obvious (or, at least, easy) to pick out the options that start Windows 95 in Normal mode.

If you are starting a Windows NT computer that you know (or suspect) has Windows 95 installed, but do not see a Windows 95 option on the boot menu; select the MS-DOS option. It may be that Windows 95 has been installed, but nobody has altered the NT boot menu to reflect this.

Logging on

As Windows 95 starts, the computer will display the Windows 95 startup logo. There is then a short time during which various system files are loaded and executed. Eventually the screen will clear and a logon prompt will appear.

The concept of logging on involves identifying yourself to the system (in this case, Windows 95). The benefit you gain from identifying yourself to the system is that personal settings (anything from colour schemes to automatic starting of applications) can then be applied. The benefit others gain from knowing it is you who is logged on is that they can allow you access to files they want you to see, or indeed deny you access to files they don't want you to see (this applies when you are part of a network – see later).

In most cases Windows 95 will request that you log on. In order
to log on, you must supply a username and a password . The
password helps to ensure that others cannot 'impersonate' you
and gain access to things that they shouldn't.

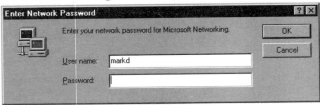

The username you choose is entirely up to you. The main restriction is that it should not already exist on the computer. In
fact, you can have several different usernames if you like, each
one with its own password.

*Enter a username and a password (make sure it is a pass-
word you will not forget). The password is not case-sensi-
tive.*

Press Enter *or click* OK

*If you have never used a graphical user interface before, 'clicking'
may require some explanation. To click something requires using
the mouse. When you move the mouse, the pointer moves accordingly on the screen. You can therefore 'point' to something on
screen with the mouse. Pressing and releasing the left mouse button will select or activate whatever you are pointing to. This is known
as 'clicking'. Clicking* OK *indicates to Windows 95 that you
accept any statement or question on the screen.*

If this is the first time a particular username has been used on
the computer, you will be prompted to type in your password
again. Re-typing your password helps to ensure that what you
thought you typed the first time is actually what you did type.
Notice that the password box displays an asterisk for each letter that is typed (so that someone looking over your shoulder
does not discover your password). It is, therefore, not easy to see

that you have typed the wrong letter and you may end up with a password that you think is 'secret' but which Windows 95 has stored as 'sercet'.

🖐 *'secret' is not a good choice of password; it is in the top five in the list of passwords that 'hackers' will try if they are trying to break into your system. Your name, your spouse's name, your children's names, your pet's name, 'password' and 'open sesame' may likewise be considered hacker-fodder.*

Windows 95 will compare the two passwords you type and, if they differ in any way, will generate an error and ask you to try again.

The password is stored (encrypted) in a file on the hard disk of the computer (the file has the extension PWL). When you log on to this computer again with that username, you must use the same password stored in the password file. If you do not enter the correct password for your username, you will see:

In this case, you must enter the correct password to log on.

Alternatively you can click [Cancel] on the logon dialog. You will be allowed to proceed, but not be logged on. Therefore will not get the benefits of any individual settings that may have been saved for you. You may also find that you have trouble accessing programs, files or printers if you are on a network.

Logging on to a network

The section above described the process of logging on to the Windows 95 computer. The discussion showed that, although it is preferable to supply a username and password, it is not compulsory. Also, it is entirely possible simply to invent a new username and password as you log on.

If you are connected to a **network**, other considerations may apply. The network may be a **workgroup** (a collection of computers of similar specification running workgroup software such as Windows for Workgroups or Windows 95), in this case Windows 95 will present its own network logon dialog. The username and password supplied will be used to check access over the network.

The network may supply documents, storage space and printers which are not at your machine. These are often called **shared network resources**. However, in order to view and use resources on the network, you may need to supply a password to the network resource. If you successfully supply the password once, Windows 95 will store the password and use it on your behalf the second and subsequent times you try to connect.

Windows 95 can be configured to log on to a network automatically on startup, in which case you should use the same username and password for Windows 95 as for the network. If you don't, you will be asked to supply both, which is tedious.

Once you have logged on, Windows 95 can re-connect to any

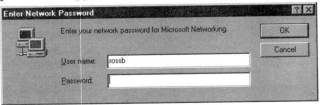

shared network resources that you have previously used. If those resources required passwords, then Windows 95 will supply them. The passwords for specific resources are stored in the password file for your username (hence the need to supply the correct name and password initially).

If you click [Cancel] while this message is displayed then Windows 95 will not reconnect to the resources and you will have to connect again yourself if you wish to use them.

If your network runs specific **client-server** network software, such as Windows NT or Novell Netware, you will almost certainly find that the network software is a lot more fussy about correct usernames and passwords. It is possible to configure Windows 95 so that it logs on the these networks directly and immediately checks the username and password against the usernames stored by the network servers. If you are using a computer configured in such a way, the logon dialog will depend on the type of network you are trying to connect to.

Hardware detection

Installing new hardware, such as a CD-ROM drive, is now much easier in Windows 95. If new hardware has been added to the computer since the last time you used Windows 95, the system should detect this and automatically try to configure the hardware for you. A dialog will appear on screen informing you of this. Hardware from most major manufacturers should be recognised by the system and setup correctly. If the system does not recognise the hardware you will be prompted with a dialog to configure the hardware.

The Welcome Screen

Once the Windows 95 loading process is complete, the Welcome Screen will appear (if you haven't previously turned it off).

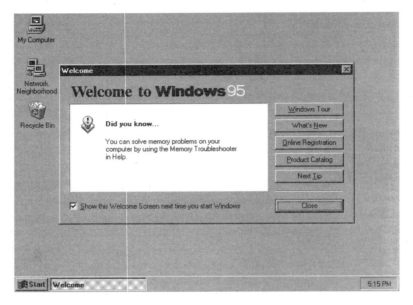

From here, you can go into a 'guided tour' or run through the new features of Windows 95 using the help system. This screen will present you with a different tip each day to help you get the most out of Windows 95. You can specify that you do not wish the Welcome screen to appear again by unchecking ☑ Show this Welcome Screen next time you start Windows.

Click

After you have closed the Welcome screen, you are left with the **desktop**:

Working with applications and data in Windows 95 requires an understanding of the desktop. It is a fundamental part of the Windows 95 interface and is discussed in the next chapter.

Summary: Starting Windows 95

- Windows 95 is an operating system and will start automatically when you turn on your computer.

- If Windows 95 is so configured, pressing [F4] will boot the previous version of DOS.

- [F8] when Windows 95 is starting will bring up the Startup menu.

- Logging on identifies you to Windows 95 and allows user-specific settings to be preserved.

- You can log on to a network when launching Windows 95.

- Windows 95 will try to detect and configure any new hardware.

3

___THE WINDOWS 95___
INTERFACE

This chapter covers:

- The desktop
- Windows 95 'tabbed' dialog boxes
- The Start menu and Taskbar
- Menus, icons and folders
- Manipulating windows and arranging icons
- Context menus

———— The Windows 95 Desktop ————

As you begin to use Windows 95, think about what you might
want to do in any particular session with your computer: start
an application, load a file, delete a file, send an e-mail message,
perform system maintenance etc. Windows 95 contains the tools
necessary to perform these tasks and the desktop is where you
start looking for them. The desktop is what initially appears on
your monitor screen after you have logged on to Windows 95.

The desktop is always there and cannot be closed or removed. You may find it helpful to think of the desktop as the highest level of the Windows 95 interface. Documents on your computer's hard disk, applications stored on a network, or devices such as printers and modems are all accessed via the desktop.

What you can see in the screenshot below is a typical Windows 95 desktop just after installation (you may have a different number of icons). Notice that it is remarkably uncluttered. After using Windows 95 for a while, your desktop may well contain many more icons (or possibly fewer) than are shown below. Later in the book, you will learn how to create your own icons on the desktop and set up your own desktop arrangement. It is possible for Windows 95 to remember the personal settings for any person who uses the computer, and to be configured with those settings whenever that person logs on.

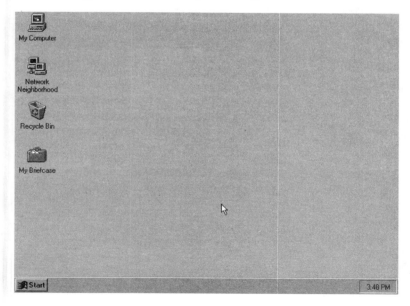

A brief Introduction to Objects

Earlier in the chapter, we mentioned some of the tasks you may have set out to achieve with your computer; opening files, launching applications etc. The tools and resources that you use to achieve these tasks, even the files you work on are represented in Windows 95 as **objects**.

Later on, we will talk about objects in more detail. For now, think of an object as a means of representing anything in Windows 95 that is distinct from anything else. A file and a modem are two separate objects. Two applications, for example, are two objects; they are both applications but they have different names and perform different tasks. Two files are two separate objects; they may both contain exactly the same text, but they have different names or are stored in different places on the hard disk (which is another object incidentally).

In many cases, one of the most important things about an object is its contents. The contents of a file is the data with which you are working, the contents of an application is the code that allows you to work with your data. Some objects contain other objects, in fact, some objects exist solely in order to contain other objects. The desktop you are looking at now contains a number of important objects, some of which contain other objects.

Now that we have established the concept of objects, how do we recognise them? In principle, an object can appear in any manner at all; in fact, some objects never apear on the screen in any form. However, the most common means of depicting an object is to use some form of **icon**. An icon is a (usually) small picture that gives a clue as to the nature of the object it represents. In many cases, the icon is accompanied by some text which gives the name of the object.

🖱 *Look at the icons on your desktop.*

Notice that each has a name and that the picture matches the name (or not, it's up to you).

> ᐁ *At this point, you may think 'I could do better than that'. You can change the icons used for the objects and even design your own - but the technique is a bit advanced for this book.*

The standard icons which appear on the desktop can be placed anywhere; they will appear on the left of the screen after Windows 95 is installed. If you move the icons their new position is used next time you start Windows 95. Two of the icons represent objects which, together, cover the entire universe (from the computer's point of view). One of them contains all the files, applications, and utilities that exist on your computer (aptly named 💻 **My Computer**); the other contains any other computer to which you are conected and is called the 🖥 **Network Neighborhood**. The other icons represent tools, the 🗑 **Recycle Bin** for holding and deleting files you no longer need and 💼 **My Briefcase** for managing files you need to work on in different locations (more on these later).

———— Using windows ————

An icon represents an object that may contain other objects. The contents of an object are displayed using a **window**. For example, a window can display a list of files on your computer's hard disk, or the data in a document such as the text in a letter.

Double-clicking an icon

You can open a window for an object by double-clicking the object's icon (this technique has been presented as a universal fact, there are a few exceptions, but you will get used to them as you experiment with Windows 95). To double-click an icon, move the mouse pointer to the icon and then click the left mouse button twice in rapid succession, without moving the mouse.

There is a logic to the concept of double-clicking. Objects such as files and computers can have actions performed on them, for example a file can be printed or deleted. Later you will see that Windows 95 can give you a list of some of the actions that an object supports, including a default action. Clicking an icon once selects that object. Double-clicking causes the object's default action to be performed on it. The default action for 🖳 My Computer is to open and display the objects it contains in a window.

🖱️ *Double-click* 🖳 *My Computer.*

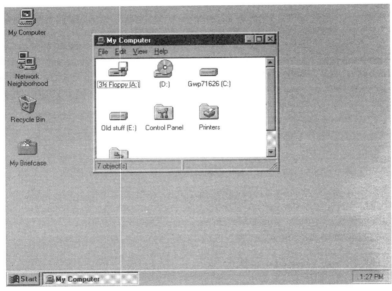

A window opens containing more icons. These icons represent other objects such as the hard and floppy drives on your computer; and folders for configuring your system, working with printers and network connections. You may well have a different set of icons from the ones shown above. (Folder icons will be explained later in the book.) Below the icons for the hard drives on your computer will be the drive letter in parentheses, e.g. (C:), as well as any name that has been assigned to the drive.

To see what is on your C: drive, double-click the icon for your C: drive.

Instead of double-clicking you could click once to select the object and then press ⎡Enter⎤. Both actions produce the same result.

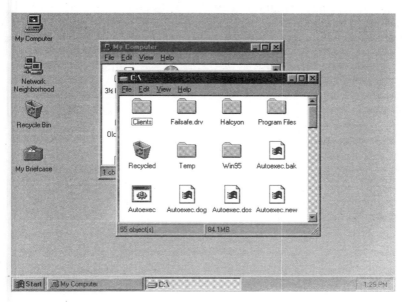

The window for the C: drive contains several different icons. By default, the icons are displayed in an orderly grid, with the icon title beneath each one. Each different icon represents a particular type of object. The C: drive window will display icons for documents, programs and folders stored at the highest level, or 'root directory' of the drive. You should see folder icons representing 'sub-directories', or lower levels of the C:\ drive, which in turn can contain other documents, programs and folders. You will see more of this structured storage later in the book.

It is important at this stage to appreciate that the window is a means of viewing the contents of the object; it is not the object itself. Windows, therefore, behave in similar ways regardless of the object they are being used to examine. It is worth while examining the behaviour of windows before going on to look at specific objects.

Moving and resizing windows

It is worth spending a little time examining some of the things you can do with a window. For this you will use the window for the C: drive, although the concepts introduced apply to all windows you will work with.

> ⟨ℐ *Some objects display themselves in windows that have different modes of behaviour. In some cases the user may choose to employ a window with different properties, the most notable example is probably the Explorer (see later).*

At the top of the window is the title bar. This identifies what the window is displaying and is usually the name of the object whose contents are being viewed. If your C: drive has a label, you will see this in the title bar, otherwise you will just see the drive letter (C:). As well as the title, the title bar also contains a number of other icons, which will be explained later in this chapter.

The title bar may be used to move a window to a new position on the screen. This is done by dragging.

👍 *'Dragging' means clicking and holding down the mouse button, then moving the mouse with the button still held down. Whatever the mouse pointer is on when you click will be 'dragged'. Dragging is very useful in many situations, such as moving objects and icons or resizing, as you will see shortly.*

🖱 *Try dragging the C: drive window around the screen by dragging its title bar.*

Notice that the mouse pointer cannot move off the screen, though parts of the window you are dragging can. Therefore, it is not possible to move the window to a position from which you cannot retrieve it (though you can get it close enough to be awkward).

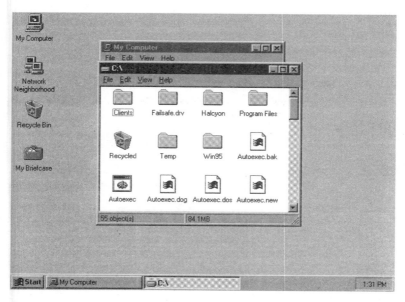

Finally, position the window centrally on the screen.

The window may well be too small to display all the icons. One solution is to change the size by dragging the window border.

Move the mouse pointer to the border of the C:\ drive window.

The mouse pointer should change shape to a double-headed arrow, e.g.

Hold down the left mouse button and move the mouse so that the window changes size.

You can move any of the window borders. To change the width and height of the window at the same time, drag the window from one of its corner areas. You can tell when the mouse is pointing to a window corner area because the mouse pointer will become a diagonal arrow.

🖱 *Drag a window by the corner until it is too small to display all its icons at the same time.*

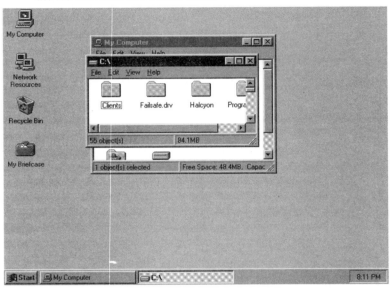

Notice that there are two **scroll bars** in the window. Scroll bars are used to scroll the window, so that what is displayed moves up, down, left or right, by clicking the buttons at either end of the scroll bar. The scroll bar on the right scrolls the window up or down, the one at the bottom scrolls left or right.

🖱 *Click the scroll bar buttons to scroll the window.*

Note that the direction in which the icons move will be opposite to the direction in which the window is being scrolled. You might find it easier to think of the process as 'panning' with a camera;

as you pan the camera (window) to the right, the objects appear to move to the left.

Clicking the buttons at the ends of the scroll bars scrolls the window by a pre-set amount. The window can be scrolled to any position you wish by dragging the **scroll button**. This is located in the scroll bar itself. The position of the button gives you an idea of what part of the available area you are looking at, if the button is towards the top of the scroll bar, you are looking at the top of the window and there may be more to see by scrolling down. The size of the scroll button relative to the size of the scroll bar itself indicates the proportion of the window you can actually see at the moment; if the scroll button occupies a quarter of the scroll bar, then you can only see a quarter of the available height (or width).

Finally, clicking in the scroll bar itself (not the scroll button) will scroll the window by a much larger amount than clicking the buttons at the ends of the bars. Typically, clicking the arrow buttons will scroll by one line (of icons or whatever) but the clicking the scroll bar will scroll by one page or 'windowful'. The direction of scrolling depends on which side of the scroll button you click. Clicking below the button scrolls down, clicking to the right of the button scrolls right etc.

 Change the size of the window and see how the size of the scroll button changes relative to the scroll bar.

Experiment with scrolling the window, use each of the methods described above in turn.

Closing windows

Closing a window removes it from view. You may be used to closing a window in order to close down an application (with all the attendent saving of data and so on), closing a window on the contents of an object usually does no more than remove the window from the desktop. To close a window, click the close button ▨ on the right of the window's title bar.

🖰   *Click* ❌ *to close the window for the C: drive.*

When you close a window, its size is remembered and will be used next time you open that window.

🖰   *Reopen the window for the C: drive.*

The window is the same size as when you closed it.

🖰   *Enlarge the window so that you can see lots of icons.*

——————————— Using Menus ———————————

A **menu** is part of the user interface to Windows 95. Put another way, menus are used to give instructions to Windows 95 and the applications you run in it. A menu is a list of commands, grouped together by category. The menus change according to the application or window you are using and, in some cases, what you are doing. Menus grouped together on a **menu bar**, which is located just below the title bar of the window in which you are working. The C:\ drive window has a standard set of menus.

The **menu titles** tell you what category the commands fall into. For example, the File menu contains commands for file and document management, such as creating new documents or opening or deleting existing documents. There is also a Close command to close the window.

🖰   *Click the File menu, i.e. click the word 'File', and examine the commands listed there.*

👆   The letter 'F' is underlined in the menu title. This indicates that you can type ⌈ Alt ⌋-⌈ F ⌋ to activate the menu.

Some commands can only be used in particular situations and will be unavailable from time to time. Such commands will appear in a different colour (sometimes known as 'greyed' or 'dimmed') and cannot be chosen.

The menu systems in Windows 95 require one click to activate them, then one more click to select a command. When one menu is visible you can simply point to another to view that one instead. As you move the mouse pointer up and down the menu (without any mouse buttons held down), the commands on the menu become highlighted as your mouse moves over them.

✍ *This behaviour differs from earlier versions of Windows and is known as Sticky Menus. Sticky menus enable you to move more quickly through the menu structure. Applications running in Windows 95 will also have sticky menus.*

To get the hang of using menus in Windows 95, you will change the way the icons are displayed using the View menu.

🖱 *Move the mouse so that you are pointing to View instead of File. There is no need to click again.*

The View menu appears. The commands on this menu are used to control what appears in the window. There are several different ways in which icons can be displayed in a window. The current arrangement is indicated by the black dot next to the option. By default icons are displayed as Large Icons. Using Small Icons lets you see more icons for a given size of window.

🖱 *Move the mouse pointer down to Small Icons.*

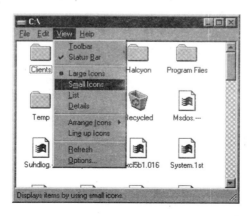

As the pointer moves over each command on the menu, notice that the command becomes selected.

🖰 *With the Small Icons command selected, click the mouse button.*

The command is performed and the window now shows small icons. These are still arranged in a grid. Have a look at the order in which the icons are arranged. The folder icons come first, followed by the files. Notice that, by default, the folders and files are sorted alphabetically by name. (Folders are covered in detail later.)

🖰 *From the View menu reset the icons to be large.*

Changing Icon Titles

An icon's title, or name, is the text below the icon. The title is part of the description of the object that the icon represents. You may change the title of the icons in a window or on the desktop without affecting what they do. For example, it is possible (but perverse) to swap the names of the Network Neighbourhood and My Computer without changing anything else about the object. To change the title of an icon, for example that of the 🖳 Network Neighborhood, click the icon once to select it, then click the text below the icon to enter **edit mode**.

👆 *If you click the text too soon after clicking to select the icon, you will open the window because you have double-clicked. Make sure you pause before clicking so that you go to edit mode.*

🖰 *Click once to select the 🖳 Network Neighborhood icon title.*

🖑 *Type in a new icon title, then press* Enter
or click the desktop to keep the change, or
Esc *to cancel and leave the title as it was.*

This procedure can be used to rename any icons, including a
file or folder. For consistency over the rest of the book, you
should leave the 🖳 Network Neighborhood icon title as it was.

🖑 *If you have changed the icon title, repeat the above steps*
to rename the icon back to 🖳 *Network Neighborhood.*

👆 Although changing the names of some objects is harmless, this is
not generally the case. Changing the name of a file object will
rename the file, and any applications that expect to find the file will
then not be able to do so.

Arranging icons

Icons can be repositioned by dragging, either on the desktop or
within a window.

🖑 *Drag the icons in the C: drive window to random positions.*

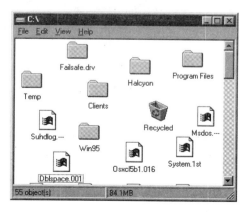

👆 *If you find that the icons can be dragged only to 'orderly' positions, or jump to new positions when you release the mouse button, then the Auto Arrange option has been turned on (see below).*

If you have many icons within a window, you may find locating a specific one easier if there is some order to the icons. Again, Windows 95 provides an easy way to do this.

Perhaps you wish to sort the icons by the size of the folder or file. To do this, you will need to choose one of the Arrange Icons options from the View menu. Menu items that provide access to **Sub-menus**, such as Arrange Icons, can be identified by the triangular symbol ▸ to the right of the item. Options that can be gouped together, such as the various ways to arrange icons, are generally placed in a sub-menu.

🖱 *Click View to select the menu then move the pointer down to Arrange Icons.*

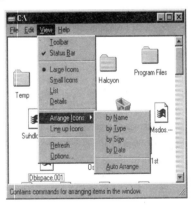

When you point to the title, the sub-menu opens shortly after.

🖱 *Choose to arrange by Size.*

You can arrange icons by Name, Type (i.e. document, program etc.), Size or Date. The Auto Arrange option will move icons into an orderly arrangement of rows and columns, but will not re-order them by any other criterion. If Auto Arrange is selected, icons will 'snap' into position when they are dragged.

There is a Line up Icons command on the context menu will also present the icons in an orderly, but not ordered, way. This is a temporary measure, however, unlike Auto Arrange. Context menus will be introduced later.

Choose by Name from the Arrange Icons submenu.

Note, again, that folder icons come before file icons. The idea here is to facilitate moving through various levels of storage.

Context menus

One of the benefits of menus in a user interface is that they are always available. It doesn't matter how you have your window scrolled or how the documents are arranged within the window, the menus are in their normal place. Menu commands tend, therefore, to provide access to features that are globally applicable (you may want to save a file you are editing from any point in the document). Cases in which the menu command applies to a specific part of the document or window usually require you to select that part first (known as the 'select then do' approach).

However, there are situations in which it would be convenient to have a menu of commands, but there is no place to put a menu bar; the desktop is a good example, it has no title bar or space for a menu.

Suppose we wanted to rearrange the icons on the desktop. There is no menu bar for the desktop, but we can get access to something called a **context menu**.

 Close any open windows so that you can see the desktop icons (remember, to close windows click ✕).

Drag the icons on the desktop to a new position.

You must use the context menu to access commands for the desktop. Context menus are activated by a right button click.

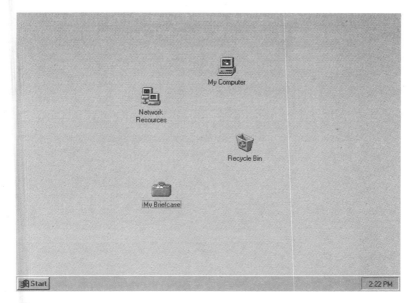

 *Right-click a blank area of the desktop.*

The desktop's context menu appears. Clicking something on the screen with the right mouse button to produce a context menu is a frequently used technique in Windows 95.

It is not quite global, there are cases where a right click produces a different effect, but it is sufficiently common to make it a useful 'rule of thumb'. The context menu contains commonly used commands, but they will apply to the particular object that was right clicked. In other words, the select then do approach has already occured, by selecting the object with the right mouse button, you have chosen the target for the menu commands. Therefore, the commands presented on the context menu are the ones most likely (in the opinion of the programmers) to be useful with that particular object. A large number of objects, particularly on the desktop, will have their own context menu.

Point to the Arrange Icons sub-menu on the context menu.

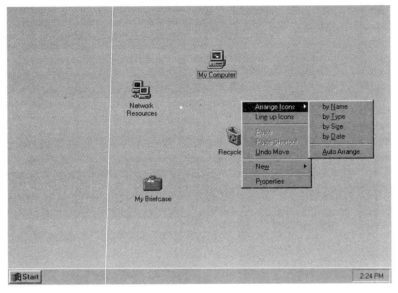

Notice that the commands on the sub-menu are the same as those you saw earlier for a window.

This time choose to arrange the icons by Type.

This takes the icons back to their default position on the desktop.

Property sheets and tabbed dialogs

Commands like 'Arrange Icons' or 'Save' are sufficiently straight-forward to require no input from the user other than choosing the command in the first place. However, there are many cases in which the exact way in which a command should be carried out needs to be specified after the command has been chosen. For example, 'Save' could be followed by questions such as 'where shall I save it?' and 'what shall I call it?' (actually, there is often a Save As option that does just this). The user is given the op-portunity of supplying this information through **dialogs**.

Dialogs are also used to present options from sources other than menus. One important use is to present what are know as **property sheets**. Properties apply to objects, they describe the way in which the object behaves. Properties can be simple and general, such as colour or name; or more complax and specific, such as whether a Virtual DOS Machine should use Fast ROM Emulation (don't worry what this is, it's just an example).

Dialogs allow users to configure a specific set of options for a wide range of commands and objects. A **tabbed** dialog is one which contains a large number of options for you to set. The options are grouped together by category so that you only see a manageable number of them at one time. Each set can be accessed by clicking a **tab** in the dialog. Tabbed dialog boxes are not new, but they are used more frequently in Windows 95 than in previous versions of Windows.

 *Right-click an empty part of the desktop.*

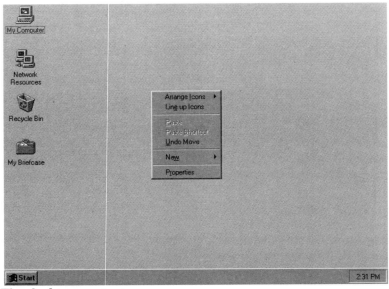

The desktop context menu appears.

The properties of the desktop object will be used to illustrate a Windows 95 tabbed dialog. Later in the book, the concept of properties will be discussed more fully. It is sufficient for now simply to use a tabbed dialog, for instance to set the desktop properties – in this case the background colour.

 *Choose the final item, Properties.*

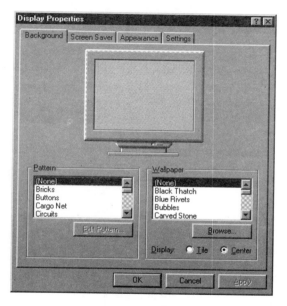

A Display Properties dialog with four tabs appears.

The tabs are 'Background', 'Screen Saver', 'Appearance' and 'Settings'. You may have a fifth tab, 'Plus!', if you have Microsoft Plus! for Windows 95 installed on your computer.

This dialog allows you to set the appearance of the Windows 95 interface and the desktop, as well as configuring screen savers and monitor settings. The first tab in the dialog is the Background tab. From here, you can choose a Pattern or Wallpaper for the desktop background. To begin with, you will change the Windows 95 colour settings, which is done from a different tab in the Display Properties dialog box.

🖰 *Click the Appearance tab in the dialog.*

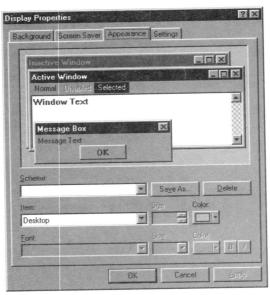

Just below the four tabs is a sample desktop with windows and a dialog box, so that you can see what the various colour schemes look like. To choose a colour scheme, you must use a **drop down list box**. These interface objects allow you to see a list of possible values and select one from the list.

🖰 *Click on the Scheme drop down list box.*

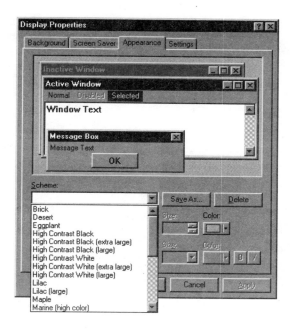

List boxes have scroll bars if there are more items in the list than can be seen, so that you can scroll to see all the permitted values. In addition, you can usually type a character on the keyboard and the list box will show you the nearest entry to what you have typed, e.g. typing P would select 'Plum'.

🖰 *Choose a scheme from the list.*

The sample desktop is redrawn using the new colour scheme.

🖰 *Try out other colour schemes until you find one you like.*

The colour schemes can be customized. For example, you may wish to change just the desktop colour for the colour scheme you choose. Notice that the 'Item' list box currently shows 'Desktop'. If you choose a different Color, it will apply to the desktop.

🖑 *Click the Color button*

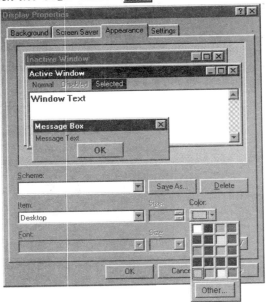

🖑 *Choose (by clicking) a colour you like from the palette.*

The sample desktop will change to show the new colour. To change the real desktop,

🖑 *Click* Apply

👆 *If you click* OK *here, the dialog closes and you must reopen it if you wish to make further changes.*

The dialog is still displayed, so that you can change other properties. You may wish to experiment with setting other Item properties, such as icon size and spacing, or caption button size (buttons such as ▬ and ✕ are caption buttons).

🖑 *Click the Background tab in the dialog box. Now click on the Tile option at the bottom of the dialog.*

Experiment with changing the Pattern and Wallpaper settings for the desktop background. Here is what Red Boxes wallpaper looks like (in black & white!):

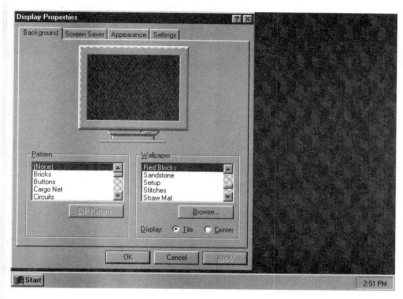

If you wish to set up a screen saver in Windows 95, click the Screen Saver tab and select one from the drop down list. A screen saver is a program which draws pictures on your screen (temporarily) after a certain period of inactivity. Screen savers were originally developed as a method of extending the life of your monitor, by preventing the same image from appearing on the monitor and 'burning in', or destroying the little dots, called pixels, which make up the screen.

✐ *Click the Screen Saver tab and experiment.*

As with the other options in the Properties dialog, you can click Apply once you have found the one you prefer.

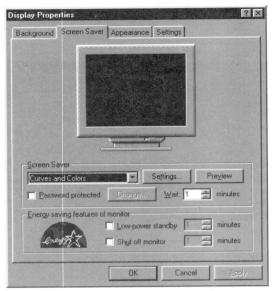

The fourth tab in the Display Properties dialog box, marked Settings, will enable you to change the settings of your monitor. It is possible to make the screen display more colours or use a higher resolution. The settings that will be available to you will depend on your hardware. Do not change the settings now unless you are confident of what your hardware allows.

When you are happy with the display properties, click

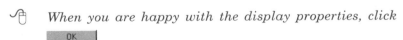

> *Be aware that Windows 95 can be configured so as to restrict the tabs that are displayed in certain property sheets. This feature is most likely to be used in large organizations in which policies for users are set and administered centrally. If, at any stage, your dialogs do not contain the tabs described in this book, contact you network administrator or whoever configured Windows 95 on your system.*

The Taskbar and Start menu

The **Taskbar** and **Start menu** are central features of the Windows 95 interface. The Start menu is a commonly used way of opening applications and documents, finding files or opening the Windows 95 help system. The Taskbar allows you to switch easily between any open applications or windows.

The Taskbar is the grey bar (or band) that runs across the bottom of the screen. At the right end of the Taskbar is a clock showing the current (system) time. At the left end of the taskbar is the Start button  which activates the Start menu.

The Start menu

Click

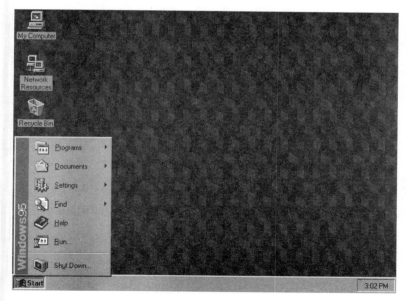

The Start menu is useful for opening application programs, documents, system utilities, the help system or shutting down Windows 95. The Start menu groups together similar programs.

🖰 *Move the mouse slowly up the Start menu.*

Notice that the Start menu is also 'sticky'.

🖰 *Point to the top item on the Start menu, 'Programs'.*

The Programs submenu will appear.

🖰 *Now move the mouse pointer over the Accessories submenu.*

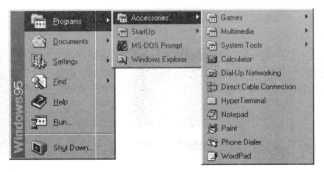

Another submenu appears! This is because the first item on the Programs submenu is the Accessories submenu. The submenu shows the Accessories that come with Windows 95 (those that have been installed, anyway).

The submenus off the Programs submenu correspond to program groups in the Windows 3.x Program Manager. If you install Windows 3.x applications using Windows 95, and the application Setup program would normally create a program group, the appropriate submenu will appear here in Windows 95.

Unlike Windows 3.x, the Start menu can have more than one level of hierachy; groups can contain other groups that contain other groups and so on. You may find this confusing at first, but you will get used to it. It also means that you can arrange a structured system with less 'clutter' on screen at any one time.

Move to the Games submenu (at the top), then click the icon for Solitaire.

Notice there is now a button for Solitaire on the Taskbar. All open applications and windows (though not dialogs) will appear in this way on the Taskbar.

You may already be familiar with this application if you have used Windows 3.x! Before rushing into a game, as this may be the first time you have worked with application windows in Windows 95, it is worth pausing to point out a few features.

The application window has a title bar with the application name in, and a grey border, which can be used to resize the window. Nothing too different from Windows 3.x here perhaps, but notice what is at either end of the title bar. On the right are three buttons, which are used to **minimise** ▬ , **maximise** ▢ or **close** ✕ the window (maximise and minimise will be discussed later).

The control menu is still at the left end of the title bar, but is activated by clicking the icon to the left of the application name.

👍   *Pressing* Alt *-* ▭ *will also activate the control menu.*

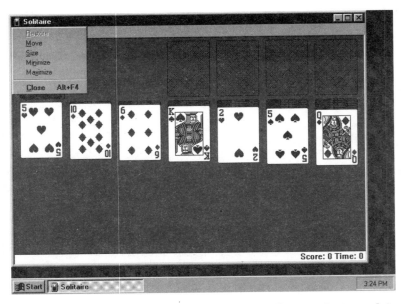

Notice that the control menu is very similar to that used in Windows 3.x.

🖱 *Put the control menu away without selecting a command, by clicking the application icon in the title bar, pressing* ⌈Alt⌉ *or pressing* ⌈Esc⌉ *twice.*

Opening another application

You may wish to run more than one application simultaneously. To try this you will use Notepad, a simple text editor used in both Windows 95 and Windows 3.x.

🖱 *Click* ▤Start *then select Notepad from the* Programs, Ac-cessories *submenu.*

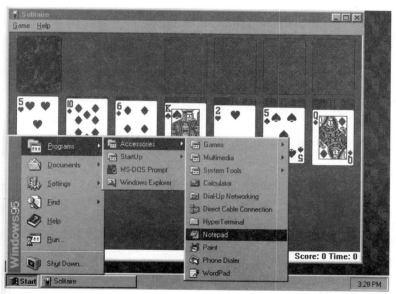

🖱 *Click to open Notepad.*

There is no need to leave Solitaire before doing this. The Start menu can be used to launch one application while another is running. Whilst in Windows 3.1 this was possible, you would first have had to switch to Program Manager. In Windows 95 the Start menu is always available without having to switch between applications, even when your current application is maximised.

Managing applications with the Taskbar

A major purpose of the Taskbar, besides giving easy access to [Start] is to simplify working with several applications simultaneously. At the moment you have two applications running; you can probably still see the Solitaire window open in the background. The Solitaire button [Solitaire] has stayed on the Taskbar, but notice that the button has now 'popped out', rather than being 'pushed in'. As you may well deduce, this indicates that Solitaire is no longer the active application.

Note that there is also a button for Notepad on the Taskbar. The button displays the contents of that application's title bar, which means that for applications such as Notepad, the Taskbar buttons also show which document is open. In this case, since you have not typed anything in and saved the document, 'Untitled' appears as the document in Notepad.

> 🔗 *This process of running more than application at the same time, known as 'multi-tasking', is significantly improved in Windows 95. Although more than one Windows application could be open at a time in Windows 3.x, one would not really do much in the background while another application was doing something in the foreground. Applications continue to execute tasks in the background in Windows 95.*

⌐🖰 *In Notepad, type in a list of the features you have noted in Windows 95.*

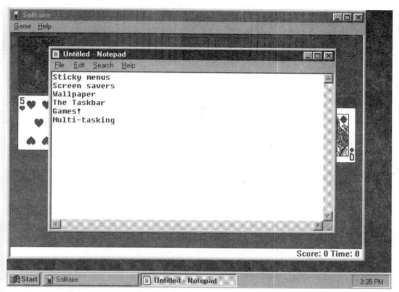

Switching between applications

There are numerous ways of switching from one application to another. Perhaps the simplest is to click on the appropriate window if it is visible in the background, as is the case for the screen shown above. Alternatively, you can use the Taskbar. To return to an application simply click its Taskbar button.

⌐🖰 *Click* 🃏 Solitaire *to go back to Solitaire.*

Another way to switch between open applications is to press Alt and Tab together. If you do this and release the keys straight away, you will switch to the previous application (repeat to switch back again). To go to any one of several open applications, hold Alt down while pressing Tab. This will allow you to move through a list of open applications and select the one you require.

— 45 —

This technique was commonly used in Windows 3.x and is still supported under Windows 95. However, you may find it easier simply to click the Taskbar.

🖑 *Try pressing* Alt *and* Tab *together to go back to Notepad.*

👈 Pressing Ctrl - Esc *has a different purpose in Windows 95 than in Windows 3.x. In Windows 95 it activates the Start menu.*

🖑 *Click* ✕ *to close Notepad. Click* No *when asked if you wish to save the changes.*

Working with documents will be covered later in the book.

Minimising and Maximising windows

Although you can use the control menu, the ▬ and ☐ buttons would be most people's choice to minimize or maximize a window.

🖑 *Click* ▬

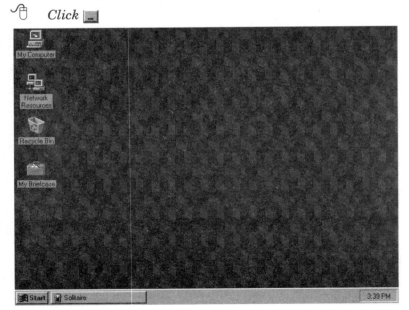

The window disappears. You may have been able to spot the window 'collapsing' to the Taskbar. This feature was added to Windows 95 so that novice users would be able to see where their window had gone.

Click

The Solitaire window has been restored.

Click ⬜ *to maximise Solitaire.*

Notice that although the window has been maximised, the Taskbar is still visible at the bottom of the screen.

Now right-click the window's title bar to produce a context menu where you click. Notice that the context menu is the same as the control menu.

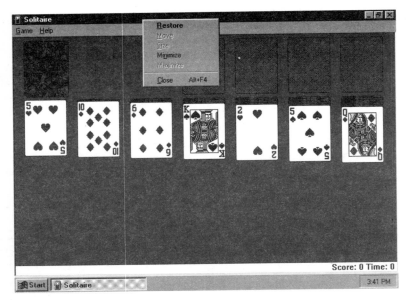

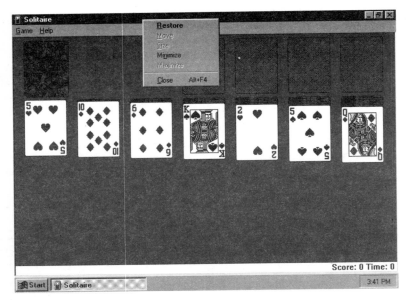 *Select Mi̲nimize from the context menu to return the application to the Taskbar.*

Application windows still have a context menu when they are on the Taskbar.

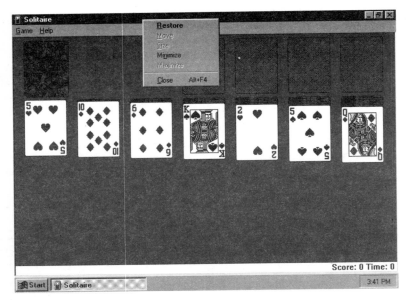 *Right-click on the Taskbar.*

Once again the control menu appears. Unless you feel you have time for a quick game, it is time to close Solitaire and move on to more edifying applications! This could be done in several ways, e.g. pressing Alt - F4 . Alternatively, if the Solitaire window was active, you could quit by selecting Ex̲it from the G̲ame menu or clicking X in the title bar. You can also quit an application directly from the Taskbar by using the context menu.

 Select C̲lose from the context menu to quit Solitaire.

– 48 –

Arranging windows

As you have seen, applications such as Notepad run in their own window, which can be maximised to full screen or minimised to the Taskbar. If you are working with more than one application, you may want to see the documents in each one at the same time. This can be done by resizing and repositioning the windows to suit, either manually or automatically.

🖰   *Click* 🔳Start *and launch Paint from the Programs, Accessories submenu.*

Paint is the Windows 95 equivalent of Paintbrush, the Windows 3.x bitmap graphics application. If the window is maximised, click 🗗 to restore the window.

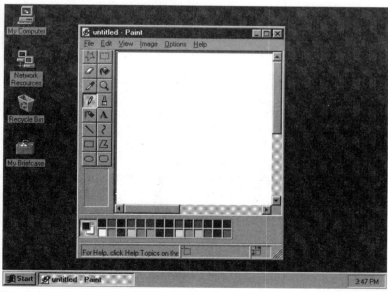

To resize the Paint window move the mouse to one of the window borders or corners so that the pointer changes to a double-headed arrow and drag.

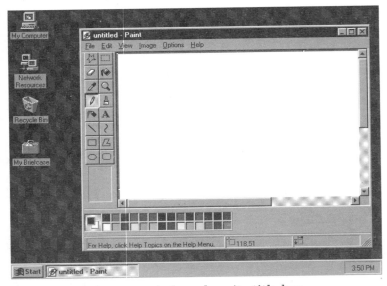

If you want to move a window, drag its title bar.

🖰 *Try sizing and moving the Paint window yourself.*

If you have several applications open you could resize and move each window so that you can see them at the same time.

🖰 *Using the Start menu, open Notepad and WordPad from the Accessories submenu. Resize and reposition the application windows.*

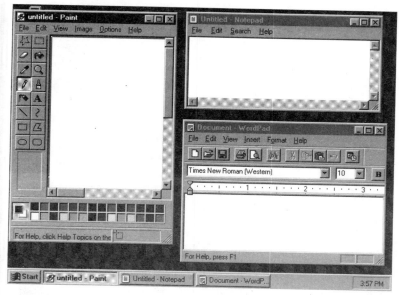

It is probably quicker, and easier, to let Windows 95 do the work for you. If you want to see all windows at the same time, you should tile the windows, either horizontally or vertically.

🖰 *Right-click a blank region of the Taskbar to invoke the context menu.*

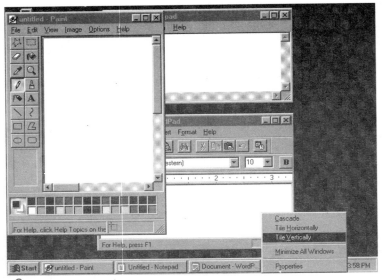

🖱 *Select Tile Vertically from the context menu.*

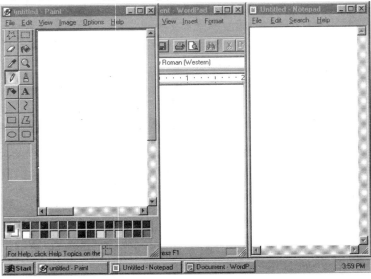

Now try Cascade from the Taskbar context menu.

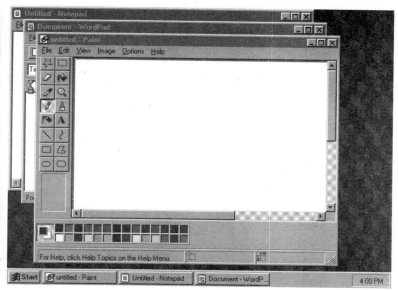

Since you can see from the Taskbar which applications are open, this may seem of little use. However, it is easy to see both the document name and application name from the title bar of the cascaded windows. The more applications and documents that are open, the smaller the corresponding Taskbar buttons and the less information the button can display.

In Windows 3.x, you would achieve similar results by starting the Task Manager and clicking the Tile or Cascade buttons. There is no Task Manager in Windows 95 since the Taskbar performs a similar, and substantially more accessible role.

If you right click the Taskbar, you can choose Minimize All Windows. This is a quick way to access the desktop. If you have minimized all open windows, you can right click the Taskbar again and choose Undo Minimize All to restore them back to their original position.

Taskbar options

The Taskbar properties control how the Taskbar and Start menu are displayed and what appears there. Although you could use the Start menu to invoke the Taskbar properties dialog box...

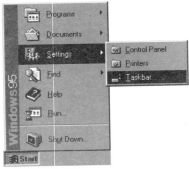

...a more general Windows 95 method for accessing the properties of an object is to right-click it.

Right-click an empty part of the Taskbar and select Properties.

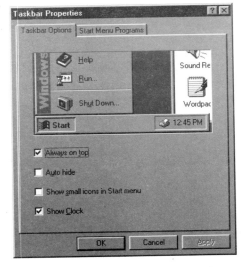

Only the Taskbar Options tab is of interest at the moment. There are four check boxes here. By default, ☑ **Always on top** and ☑ **Show Clock** are selected. If you change one of the four check boxes, the sample area in the dialog changes to show you the effect.

🖎 *Change the check boxes. Try to spot the differences in the sample area.*

The first two options may require some explanation. If ☑ **Always on top** is checked, the whole of the Taskbar is always visible, even if a window has been positioned on top of the Taskbar. The lower right corner of the sample area should illustrate this when you toggle ☑ **Always on top**.

Now have a look at ☐ **Auto hide**.

🖎 *Check ☐ **Auto hide** and click Apply.*

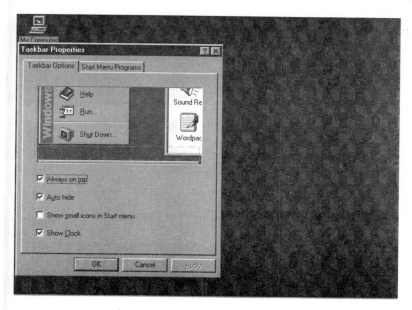

You should be able to see that the Taskbar has disappeared from the sample area. However, it is worth applying the option to appreciate the effect fully.

 *Click* OK

The Taskbar is still there, but has been hidden. Any time you want to use it, for example to run a program from the Start menu, simply move the mouse pointer to where the Taskbar ought to be. Hey presto, it reappears!

Move the mouse away again and the Taskbar disappears again. For the remainder of the book it is recommended that you set the Taskbar options so that ☑ **Always on top** is checked and ☐ **Auto hide** is unchecked.

Set these options now.

Moving and resizing the Taskbar

The Taskbar does not have to appear at the bottom of the screen. If you wish you can move the Taskbar to the top, left or right edges of the screen as well. This is done by dragging the Taskbar (click an empty part of the Taskbar for this) to the required position. While dragging the Taskbar, a fuzzy line will appear when you have dragged it to a permitted position.

Try this now.

👆 *The Taskbar will always occupy all of whichever screen edge it is on.*

If you wish to change the height/width of the Taskbar, simply move the mouse to the inner edge until it changes shape to a thin double-headed arrow, then drag to the required size.

Experiment with moving and resizing the Taskbar, then leave it positioned along the bottom edge.

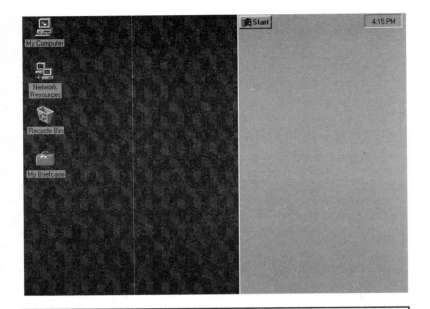

Summary: The Windows 95 Interface

- The Desktop is the centre of activity in Windows 95.
- Objects represent virtually anything you might use in Windows 95.
- The contents of objects are viewed in windows.
- You can change the appearance of the desktop by right-clicking it and choosing <u>P</u>roperties from the context menu.
- The Taskbar displays a button for each application you are running to enable you to switch easily between them.
- The Taskbar can be moved to a different edge of the screen and can be resized.
- Icons on the Desktop can be moved, arranged and renamed.

4

CREATING
—— DOCUMENTS ——
AND FOLDERS

This chapter covers:
- Creating new documents with right-click
- Renaming documents
- Creating folders
- Moving documents and folders
- Deleting documents and folders

—— Creating New Documents ——

Windows 95 is sometimes described as being 'document-centred' or 'infocentric'. This means that, as a user, your activity is centred around creating, opening and editing documents. In this context, a document is an object that contains data, which could be text, graphics, a spreadsheet, indeed anything which can be processed by an application program. Less emphasis is placed on starting specific application programs. Indeed, some documents may be opened using any of several applications.

Creating a new document with right-click

Creating new documents is made easy by the context menus.

🖱 *Right-click the desktop.*

🖱 *Choose New from the menu.*

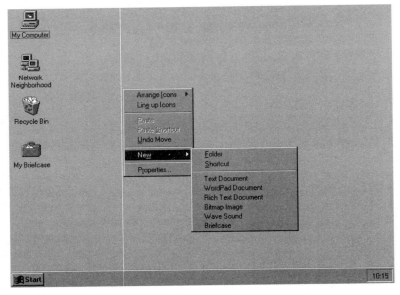

You can now choose a type of document to create. The items on this menu are dictated by the software that you have installed. For example, you may also see Word 6.0 Document, Powerpoint 4.0 Presentation or Excel 5.0 Spreadsheet if you have these products installed. You may also find that you do not have Rich Text Document if you have not installed WordPad or do not have Wave Sound if you have not installed the Media Player.

Notice that this reinforces the infocentric approach. Instead of starting a specific application and selecting a File, New option, you choose to create a document then decide what type it will be.

Choose Text Document

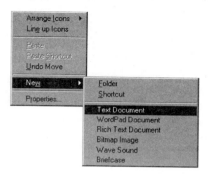

When you select the option, a new document icon appears on the desktop:

The New option is available from the context menu of folder and drive windows, so you can create new documents (or folders) anywhere in your storage structure.

Renaming a new document

The document appears on the desktop with the default name of New Text Document. You can type in a different name for the document here if you wish.

Long filenames

A document is saved as a file on a hard disk or floppy disk. One of the features of Windows 95 is that filenames can have up to 255 characters, including spaces. The characters \ ? : * " < > | are not permitted in filenames.

🖱 *Type a different name for your file.*

When you press enter or click somewhere else on the screen, Windows 95 will accept your new name and display the new icon with the name underneath. You can now move the icon to another place on the desktop if you want to keep things tidy.

The document you have created is empty.

🖱 *Double click the document icon to open the new document you have created.*

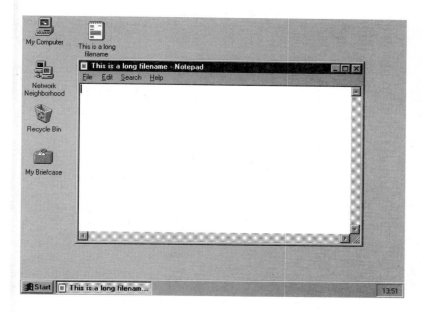

Notice that the text document automatically opens in the application program, Notepad. By default, Windows 95 **associates** text documents with the application Notepad (though you can change this if you wish).

🖑 *Type some text in the document, then click ❌ to close the Notepad window and hence the application itself.*

A general rule in Windows applications is that you will be prompted to save any changes you have made to a document when closing it, if the changes have not been saved already.

🖑 *Save the changes to your document when prompted.*

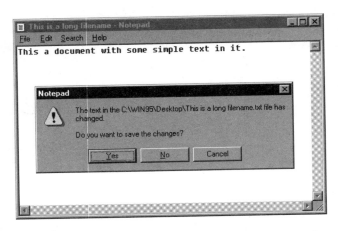

In this example, you right-clicked the desktop to create a new document. You will find that you can create a new document using the same method anywhere that you are allowed to store a file. Later, you will work with more documents, using the word processor application WordPad and the graphics application Paint.

Renaming an existing document

You may want to change the name of a document after you have created it, or you may even have tried to change the name when you created it and accidentally clicked somewhere else!

🖱 *Click the icon on your desktop for the text document you have just created.*

The document you have clicked becomes selected, but you still cannot change the name.

🖱 *Click the name of the selected icon.*

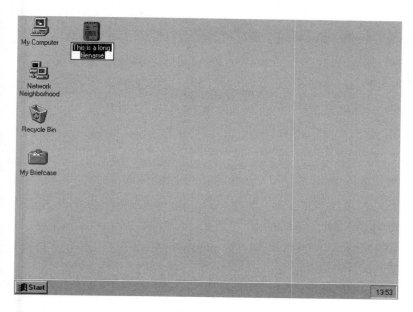

This time the name of the icon (which is also the name of the document) can be changed. If you make a mistake at this stage pressing will return the document name to what it was before you started editing it.

Type a different name for your document.

This method for changing the name of a document can be applied to nearly all of the icons that appear in Windows 95 – even My Computer! A document is one of the many objects you work with in Windows 95, as is My Computer. As mentioned earlier, the icons on the desktop represent some of these objects. Each object has a set of properties, such as its name, size, location or even icon.

Creating Folders

When you have a lot of documents on your desktop, you will probably want to group them together to make it easier to find them. Windows 95 uses folders to do this. Folders are objects that are designed to contain other objects (even more folders). They are useful for organizing and structuring the storage of other objects in your computer. Folders are analogous to directories in MS-DOS.

Creating new folders is done using a technique similar to the one used to create new documents.

Right-click the desktop and choose New from the menu.

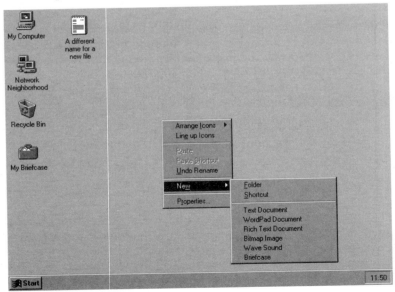

Choose Folder from the sub-menu.

This time you get a Folder icon on the desktop. Again, you can change the name of the new folder if you want to.

Type in a name for the folder.

The new Folder you have created has no documents in it yet.

Open the new folder (double-click or use the context menu)

A folder can contain documents and other folders. Next, you will create a new document in your new folder.

🖑 *Right-click the background in your folder window and choose New, Text Document.*

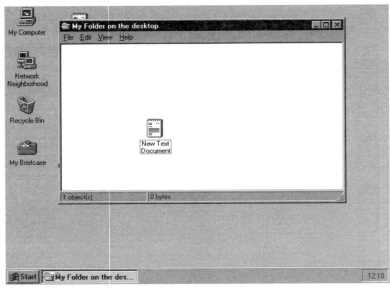

—— Moving Documents and Folders ——

Now that you have created a folder, you will probably want to put some of your other documents into it. As with many other tasks in Windows 95 this can be achieved using **drag and drop**.

Click a document on the desktop and drag it into the folder window. You may need to move the folder window first.

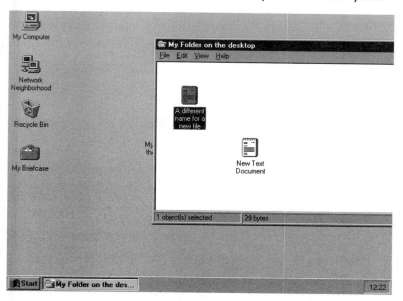

The document has now been moved into the folder. The drag and drop process will automatically copy rather than move if the source and the destination are on different disks. You can force drag and drop to copy, rather than move, by holding down Ctrl and to move instead of copy by holding down Shift.

A more convenient means of doing this is to use the right mouse button.

🖱 *Drag the document back on to the desktop using the right mouse button.*

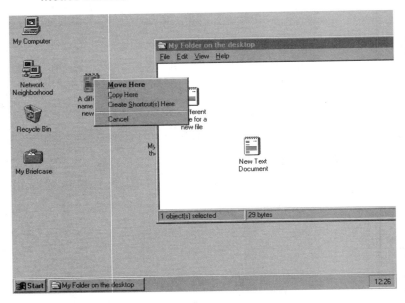

When you drop the document, a context menu appears to allow you to choose whether to copy or move the document. Notice that the default option appears in bold.

🖱 *Choose Copy Here to copy the document onto the desktop.*

This illustrates that the target folder does not need be open, the icon is enough to identify the object.

🖱 *Close the folder window.*

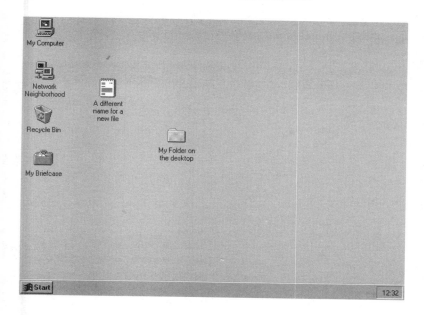

Using the right-click and drag method, you can also make a copy of a document in the same folder.

Moving and copying documents on the desktop obeys the same rules as for folders.

> ☞ *The reason for this is that the desktop is itself is a folder in 🖳 My Computer, but the window onto the desktop folder has very different properties from the window onto a normal folder.*

Make a copy of a document on the desktop with right-click and drag.

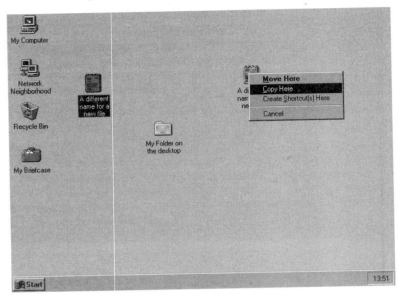

The document name is changed to avoid having two documents with the same name in a folder.

You can move and copy folders in the same way as documents.

——————— Deleting a document ———————

One way to delete documents and files is to select the file and then press [Delete]. Rather than deleting the file straight away, the file is sent to the 🗑 'Recycle Bin'.

The Recycle Bin

The 🗑 Recycle Bin is a container for all files which you wish to delete. A file which has been put in the 🗑 Recycle Bin can be deleted automatically, deleted manually at a later time or restored, if you wish to keep the file after all.

🖱 *Select the document copy you have created and press* [Delete]

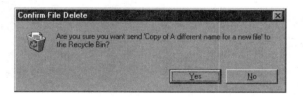

This confirmation dialog will appear every time you use this method to delete. Notice that you are 'sending the document to the 🗑 Recycle bin'.

🖱 *Click*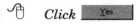

When the 🗑 Recycle Bin contains files, the icon changes – the empty bin becomes full 🗑!

A better way to delete files is to drag them into the 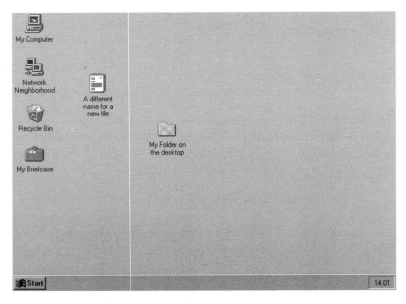 Recycle bin yourself.

Drag the original document into the Recycle Bin.

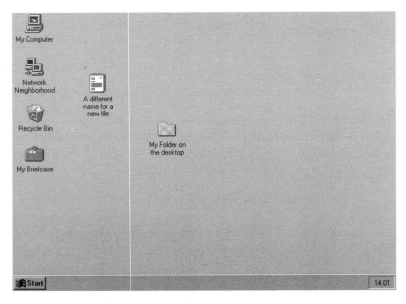

This time you are not asked to confirm the delete.

If fact, you may suspect that the Recycle bin is behaving in a similar way to a folder, in which case, you would be correct. Like the desktop, the Recycle bin is a folder that behaves in a special way. What happens to a document once it is moved to the Recycle bin, and how to recover files from the Recycle bin, will be covered in a later chapter.

Summary: Creating Documents and Folders

- The context menu enables you to create new documents and folders.

- Documents and folders can be moved with drag and drop.

- Drag and drop with the right mouse button presents a context menu on the drop action.

- Documents can be deleted by selecting and pressing ⌫ or by dragging them into the 🗑 Recycle Bin.

5

APPLICATIONS IN WINDOWS 95

This chapter covers:
- Using application programs
- WordPad – a Windows 95 word processor
- Paint – a Windows 95 graphics package
- Opening and Saving documents

Windows 95 comes with several useful application programs built in. This chapter will show you how to launch and use these applications. While no two applications have exactly the same user interface, these applications are used in much the same way as the many applications you can buy for Windows 95. In particular, the look and feel of the interface (the menus, dialogs etc.) should be consistent between all Windows 95 applications.

There are many ways of launching applications in Windows 95. The Start menu, which you will use again here, has been covered already. More techniques for launching applications will be covered later in the book.

WordPad

WordPad is a simple word processing application that can be used to produce letters, memos and other small business documents. WordPad has more formatting control than a simple text editor such as Notepad, but is not as powerful as some more fully featured word processors such as Word for Windows.

By now, you should find that many of the techniques you are going to use in WordPad should be quite familiar to you. This is one of the advantages of using a consistent environment like Windows 95.

Use the Start menu to launch WordPad from Programs, Accessories.

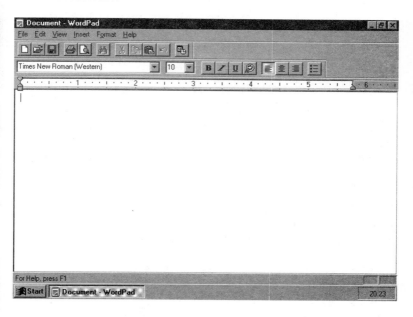

The WordPad screen

When you first open the WordPad application you should be presented with a screen like the one on the previous page.

In the window's title bar you will see the title of the current document (if your document has not yet been saved this will say 'Document') and the application name. Below the menu bar of WordPad are the Toolbar and the Format Bar. Both feature a number of buttons found in other Microsoft applications which allow shortcut access to certain application functions. The toolbar, for example, contains **file new** ☐ **open** ☞ and **save** 🖫 buttons while the format bar includes buttons for **bold** **B** **italic** **/** and **underline** **U** formatting.

Now to type in some text. Write a short letter to someone.

🖱 *Type in your address, the date and the text of your letter.*

Document - WordPad

File   Edit   View   Insert   Format   Help

Times New Roman (Western)   10   B / U

Oxford Computer Group
Wolsey Hall
66 Banbury Road
Oxford
OX2 6PR

7th July 1995

Dear Bill,

Re. Windows 95. Love the product, any chance of a T-shirt?

Best wishes,

M. S. Doss

For Help, press F1

Start   Document - WordPad   20:37

Now for some formatting. The address should be right aligned.

🖐 *Drag the mouse over the lines of the address to select them. Now click the Align Right button* ▤

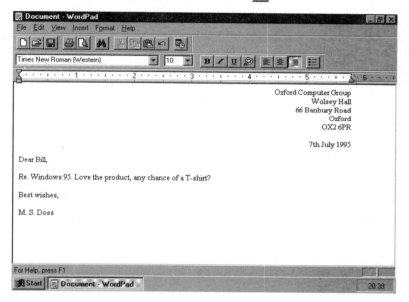

Saving files

When Save <u>A</u>s is selected from the <u>F</u>ile menu (or the  button is clicked to save a file for the first time) you are presented with a standard Save As dialog.

🖐 *Click* ▤

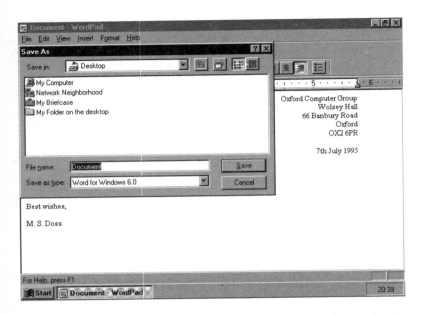

This dialog is used to save your work, giving you the option to choose where to save the document, including in another directory or on another drive. Whichever location is displayed here is where the document would be saved. Currently the dialog is displaying what is on the desktop. However, you should consider where to save your document. To keep things tidy, you could put it in the folder you created earlier on the desktop.

Double-click the icon for your folder.

Note that you can use the 'Save in:' pull down list at the top of the dialog to change location.

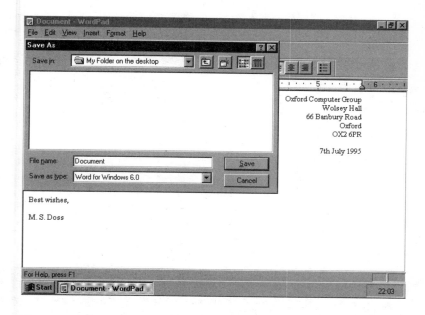

There are also a number of extra file manipulation options, accessed via context menus or buttons in the dialog.

Button	Function
	Accesses the parent of the current folder.
	Creates a new sub-folder inside the current folder.
	Displays files by name only.
	Displays all file details and enables sorting by each parameter.

If you point to the buttons with the mouse a 'tooltip' appears, indicating what each button does.

WordPad supports three document formats: Word 6 document, rich text and text only (including DOS text). The default type is

Word 6. You can specify the type of document when saving an existing document or creating a new one.

Type	Description
Text Only	A file containing no formatting or pictures. Suitable for reading into any text editing program. [Note that the file is saved as ANSI not ASCII. This will probably only matter if you have used special characters.]
Rich Text	A file with formatting and pictures. Suitable for reading into most word processing applications.
Word 6	A file containing formatting instructions for reading into Microsoft Word 6.

Type in a suitable name, e.g. 'Letter to Bill', then save the document to the folder using the default document type.

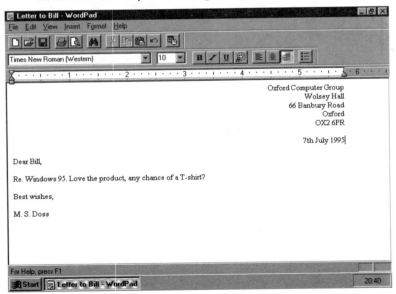

———— File Management ————

Menu commands

The WordPad File menu contains standard file manipulation commands, i.e. New, Open, Save and Save As. Print commands are also included in this menu, as well as Exit to quit the application. An increasingly common feature of File menus in applications, which is present in WordPad, is a Most Recently Used file list which allows easy access to the last four files used.

Creating a new file

A new file can be created via the File menu or by clicking the button. You are then presented with a choice of document types.

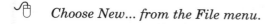 *Choose New... from the File menu.*

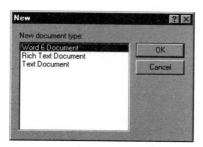

 *Select* **Rich Text Document**, *then click* OK.

Type in a list of features you have seen in Windows 95.

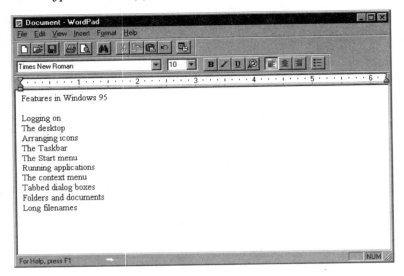

Printing files

Printing a document from WordPad is an easy task. When Print is selected from the File menu a dialog appears containing print options such as the number of copies or the page range to be printed. This dialog is fairly simple to use and contains many useful options, such as which printer to use, which pages to print (print range) and number of copies. Further dialogs are accessible to control printer parameters.

WordPad includes two buttons on the toolbar enabling shortcut printing functions. When clicked, the 🖨 button will print one copy of the entire document and will not open dialogs to control printing parameters. The 🔍 button is used to enter the print preview screen.

———————— Editing documents ————————

Menu options

WordPad's Edit menu contains an Undo command, described below, and Cut, Copy, Paste, Paste Special, Link and Paste Link commands, for controlling the Windows 95 clipboard.

Find and Replace options are also included within the Edit menu. WordPad has a Find button 🔍 on the toolbar which calls up the Find dialog. An Insert menu (detailed later) is used to insert objects.

Undo

The Undo command will in most cases reverse the last action you took. For example, if you have just deleted a large section of text, then decide you want to get the text back, you would use the Undo command. The undo command can be accessed via the Edit menu or by the keyboard shortcut [Ctrl]-[Z]. WordPad's toolbar contains an undo button 🔙 as well.

⌐🖑   *Choose Undo from the Edit menu.*

The last bit of text you typed in is removed.

⌐🖑   *Click* 🔙 *or press* [Ctrl]-[Z]

Undoing a second time puts the text back (it undoes the undo!)

Cut, copy, paste

These three commands can be used to move data around within a document or transfer data between documents and even applications. For example, you may want to take a picture from one document and put it into another, such as a report in a word processor.

The Cut and Copy commands place the data, such as a picture, in a temporary storage place, called the 'clipboard'. The Paste commands takes the data from the clipboard and puts it in your chosen location in the document. The Cut command will remove the data from the original location, whereas the Copy command leaves the data in place.

These commands can be activated via the Edit Menu or short-cut keys [Ctrl]-[X] [Ctrl]-[C] and [Ctrl]-[V] respectively. WordPad also allows these commands to be accessed via the cut ✂ copy 📄 and paste 📄 buttons on the toolbar or by right-clicking the document area to call up a context menu.

View options

The view menu

WordPad's View menu is a new development which allows the user to toggle the presence of the Toolbar, Format Bar, Ruler and Status Bar in the document area.

There is also an Options command which allows you to set default viewing settings and word wrap options.

Setting view options

Clicking on the Options command in the View menu accesses
the Options dialog which itself consists of six tabbed dialogs.

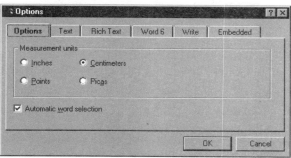

The first of these tabs (above) allows you to toggle your desired
units of measurement and whether you require automatic word
selection (which highlights one word at a time as you drag the
mouse over the text). The remaining five allow default word wrap
and viewing parameters to be set for different text types.

🖰 *Click the Word 6 tab.*

The left-hand section of the tab allows you to choose between
No Wrap, Wrap To Window and Wrap To Ruler. The right-hand
section contains check boxes to enable or disable the Toolbar,
Format Bar, Ruler and Status Bar.

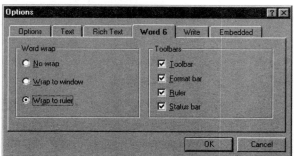

———————— Inserting items ————————

The insert menu

WordPad's Insert menu is another new development and contains just two commands. One to insert Date and Time and the other to insert a New Object.

Date and time

As the name suggests this option calls up a dialog enabling the insertion of date and time into the document in a selection of standard formats. This dialog can also be accessed by clicking the 🖼 button on the Toolbar.

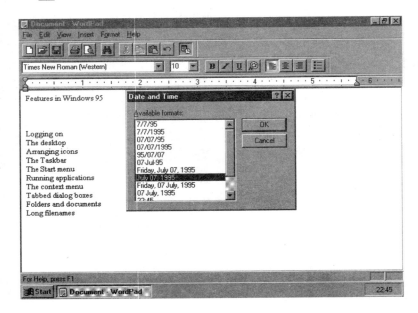

🖰   *Put a few blank lines beneath the first line, position the
     cursor in the middle of the gap and click* 🔲

🖰   *Choose the date format that you prefer.*

New object

When this option is clicked an Insert Object dialog appears. An
object is some data from another Windows application, such as
a Paint picture or a chart from a spreadsheet, which is contained
in the document. Option buttons allow you to create a new object, in which case you must choose which application to create
the object with, or create an object using data stored in a file on
disk.

There is also a check box to indicate whether the object should
be displayed within the document in icon form.

—————————— Formatting ——————————

The format menu and toolbar buttons

The Format menu is also new to WordPad and contains Font,
Bullet Style, Paragraph and Tabs commands used to format your
document. There are also toolbar buttons to apply bold 🔲 italic
🔲 and underline 🔲 formatting.

🖰   *Select the heading in the first line, then click* 🔲

Changing Font

Selecting Font from the Format menu calls up a fairly standard Font dialog which allows you to change Font, Font style and Size. WordPad also allows you to toggle Strikeout and Underline effects as well as choosing the Color from a pull-down menu (a colour palette can also be accessed by clicking 🖉 on the Format Bar). A further innovation is the ability to select different language scripts from a pull down menu. The effect of any alterations are previewed in a sample window.

🖑 *With the heading still selected, choose Font... from the Format menu.*

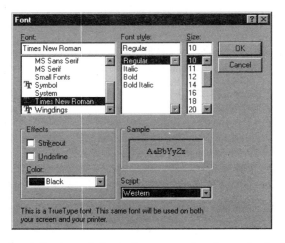

The desired font and font size can also be selected from pull down menus on the Format Bar.

🖑 *Increase the size of the font for the heading text to 14 point and click* OK

Bullets

A Bullet Style toggle exists on the Format menu which auto-matically inserts bullet point markers at the head of each new paragraph. This toggle can also be switched using the ▤ button on the Format Bar.

🖱 *Select the list of features and click* ▤

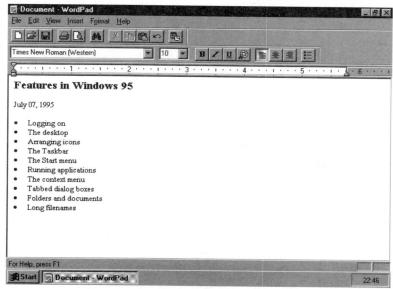

The formatting is now complete. However, there are other set-tings you may wish to consider.

Paragraphs

Selecting the Paragraph option from the Format menu reveals a dialog that allows you to alter the Left, Right and First Line paragraph indentations. There is a pull-down menu to select

Left, Right and Centre Alignment. The Format Toolbar also has buttons to select left ≣ centre ≣ and right ≣ alignment. However, full justification is not offered.

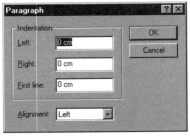

Indentation and hanging paragraphs can also be applied by moving the indent markers on the ruler. The line indent marker is represented by a downwards pointing triangle at the left of the toolbar. The left indent marker is an upwards pointing triangle at the left of the toolbar. The right indent marker is an upwards pointing triangle on the right of the toolbar. The first line and left indent markers can be moved simultaneously by dragging the small box below the left indent marker.

Setting Tabs

When Tabs is selected a Tabs dialog appears giving you control over the position of Tab locations.

Tabs can also be set by positioning the mouse pointer in the ruler and clicking. WordPad only allows you to use left tabs.

Opening files

You can open a file by clicking Open in the File menu. However, WordPad includes a standard toolbar, so a file can also be opened by clicking the 🖻 button.

🖑 *Click* 🖻 *and Look in your folder on the desktop.*

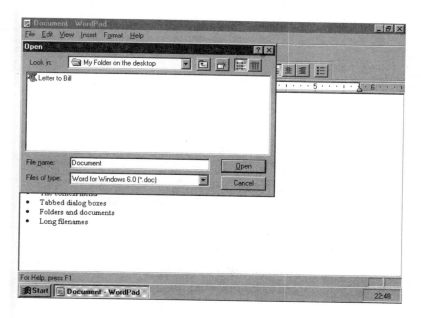

☜ *Context menus can be displayed by right-clicking the background in the Open dialog. These include some options which are not accessible via the buttons. For example if you have deleted a file and wish to retrieve it, a right-click in the file list window will enable the Undo Delete function. Icon size can also be adjusted from the context menu by selecting View.*

🖰 *Open the letter you created earlier.*

When you click ▨ Open WordPad will prompt you to save the changes to your current document. This is because only one document at a time can be open in WordPad.

🖰 *Save the changes to your feature list into you r folder on the desktop.*

You will use this letter again in the next section.

Transferring document data — ___ Scraps and the Clipboard

Desktop scraps

If you wish to re-use part of a document, you can create a 'scrap' on the desktop. To do this, select the text or graphic required and simply drag the selection to the desktop. This will create a new file with the data in it. The file is stored in the Desktop folder. To put the data into another document, simply drag the scrap icon from the desktop into the document. This will work as long as the target document 'understands' the scrap data, for example you cannot put a scrap from WordPad into Paint.

Drag and drop

🖰 *Click ▣ to restore the WordPad window and scroll so that you can see the address.*

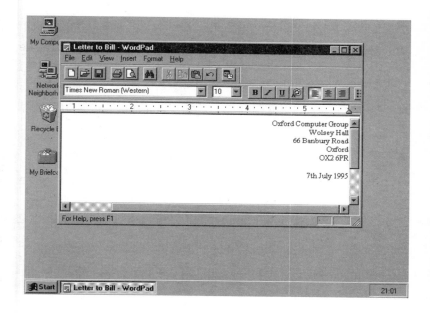

If you need to write lots of letters you may get bored typing in your address all the time. Using a scrap containing your address will help.

🖱 *Select your address in the letter, then drag it on to the desktop.*

When you let go of the mouse button the scrap is created. Notice that the icon title tells you the original application and in this case the first few words of the address.

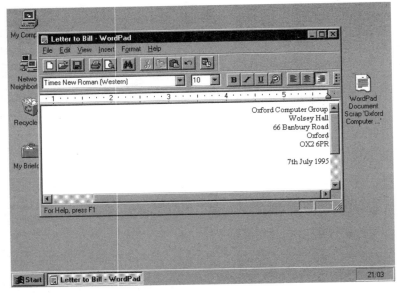

🖱 *Now start a new rich text document in WordPad.*

This will be another letter.

🖱 *Drag the address scrap from the desktop into the new document.*

Notice that the text alignment has been copied across.

🖱 *Press* Enter *then click* ▤ *to left align the remainder of the text. Write a brief letter to a recipient of your choice.*

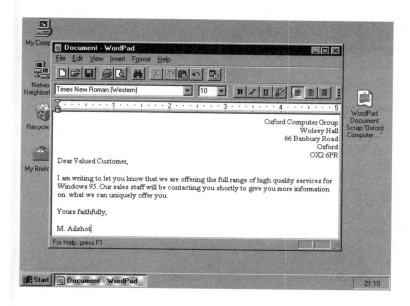

Copy and paste

You have just created a WordPad scrap by dragging on to the desktop. This is only possible because WordPad supports a technique called 'OLE drag and drop'. There is another way of creating a scrap for applications which do not support this technique – copy and paste using the clipboard.

The clipboard is a general Windows technique of transferring data from one location to another, either in the same document or between two documents, possibly of different type. It is a 'temporary storage space' for all kinds of data.

It would be a nice touch to sign your letter instead of just typing your name.

– 97 –

Paint

Paint is a bitmap graphics application which comes with Windows 95.

🖱 *Use the Start menu to launch Paint and maximize its window.*

To draw something you must select the appropriate tool from the toolbox on the left of the window. Each tool has a tooltip describing its function. Colours can be chosen from the palette at the bottom of the window.

🖱 *With the 🖉 tool selected, drag the mouse to write your signature.*

You need to select your signature before putting it on the clipboard.

🖰 *Click* 🔲 *and using the mouse drag a box enclosing your signature.*

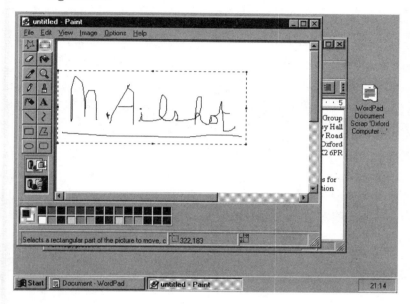

This action selects your signature.

🖰 *Right-click inside the selected area or take the Edit menu, then select Copy.*

Your signature is now on the clipboard and could be inserted into lots of other documents using the Paste command. The signature will stay on the clipboard until you put something else there, or shut down Windows 95.

🖱 *Close Paint and do not save the changes.*

Now to put your signature into a scrap on the desktop.

🖱 *Right-click the desktop and choose* <u>P</u>*aste.*

A new icon, Scrap, appears. This contains the signature.

🖱 *Now drag your signature scrap from the desktop and drop it into the WordPad document at the appropriate place.*

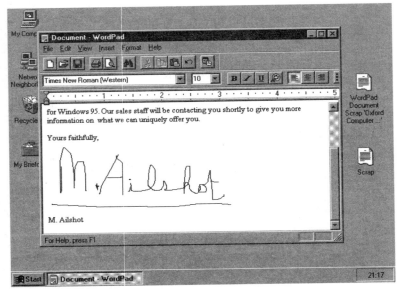

🖱 *Close WordPad, saving your letter if you wish.*

Summary: Applications in Windows 95

- WordPad is a word processor that you get with Windows 95.

- The Wordpad screen contains many standard Windows 95 features.

- Text, Rich Text and Word 6 file formats are supported by Wordpad.

- Many formatting features can be accessed from a toolbar as well as through menu options.

- Default viewing settings and format options can be set.

- The Open and Save dialog boxes allow you to navigate around My Computer.

- Documents can be saved to and opened from many locations.

- The clipboard is a general way of moving or copying data, within a document or from one to another.

- Scraps containing frequently used data can be stored and reused in other documents.

- You can create and edit bitmap graphics in Paint.

6

OBJECTS

This chapter covers:
- What is an object?
- Why use objects?
- Object properties
- A few important objects

Introduction to objects

What is an object?

We introduced the basic concept of objects earlier in the book. This chapter expands on the idea and looks at object **properties** in detail.

An object is a generic way of referring to anything that exists in Windows 95. Every document, folder, computer, printer etc. is an object. Every object is distinct from every other object, though objects may be of the same type (files, folders etc.).

One of the advantages of an **object oriented** approach like this is that all objects have certain attributes in common. One such attribute is a list of **properties**. Properties describe the way that the object appears to the outside world. Some properties are common to most objects; the name, for example, is a common property. Other properties are specific to certain types of object; only MS-DOS programs are likely to have a Quick Edit property. Changing the properties of an object changes the way it behaves in the Windows 95 environment.

You have already seen that folders can contain other folders. This is a specific example of a general principle called **containment**. Objects can contain other objects. For instance, the object that represents your computer contains all the disk drive objects and the disk drive objects contain folder objects (amongst others.

Why use objects?

By using objects to refer to all of the parts of the computer system, the interface becomes easier to use. Once you learn how to perform an action on one object, if that action is supported by another object, then the same technique will work. An example of this is that you can open any document by right-clicking it and choosing Open from the context menu.

Placing one object inside another makes things easier to organise and structure.

The advantages of objects apply to more than just the interface. Because all objects are defined using standard rules, it is very easy to introduce new objects into the environment. This makes life easy for application writers when supplying new applications for Windows 95.

Viewing objects

🖱 *Open* 🖳 *My Computer (e.g. using the context menu, or by double-clicking).*

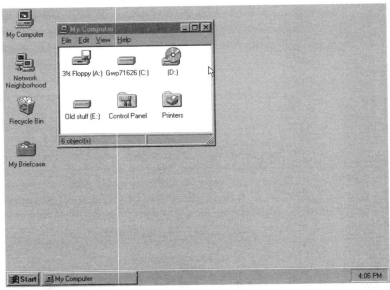

Inside the object that represents your computer are all your drives, including CD-ROMs and floppy drives.

🖱 *Open your C: drive.*

Notice that your C: drive contains lots of folders (you will have your own folders in the window – not necessarily the ones shown opposite, top) but also contains documents and the 🗑 Recycle Bin. You may also notice that as you open each object, such as the C: drive, the contents are displayed in a separate window. You can change this behaviour.

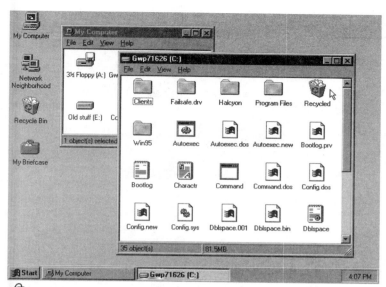

Select the <u>V</u>iew menu.

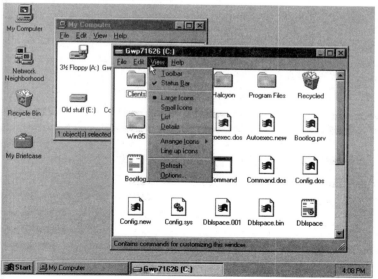

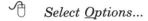 *Select Options...*

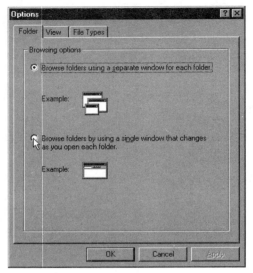

The Folder tab contains the option for allowing you to view the
contents of all the folders using the same window.

*Select the single window option and try it out by opening a
folder, e.g. Windows.*

*Repeatedly pressing the backspace key moves up through the folder
hierarchy (closing any windows that were opened, depending on
the browsing options you have taken), until you reach the top level.
In this case, the top level is ▣ My Computer – so you can't get
back up to the desktop this way.*

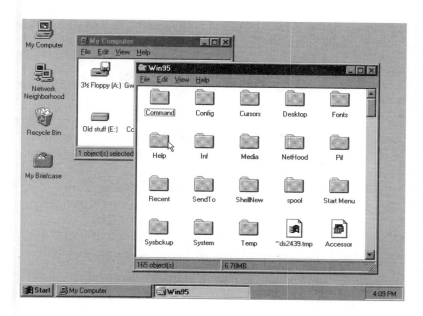

----------------- **Properties** -----------------

We introduced the concept of properties earlier. The properties of an object describe it to the outside world. For instance, documents might have a date and time of creation, a document name and size, and perhaps whether or not the document is read-only or hidden. Your computer's hard disk drive will have a changing amount of used space and free space, and possibly a disk label.

Some properties can be changed directly, the name of a document, for example. Other properties are changed indirectly, the amount of free space on a drive will change as you copy, move, create or delete files on it. Some objects have properties that cannot be changed at all (from Windows 95's point of view), the total amount of space available on a given physical disk, for example. Properties that cannot be changed or that are changed indirectly are called **read-only**; those that can be changed are know as **read/write**.

> *You may find that some people (probably programmers) refer to get and set in relation to properties. Get refers to reading, set to writing a property.*

Right-click a document.

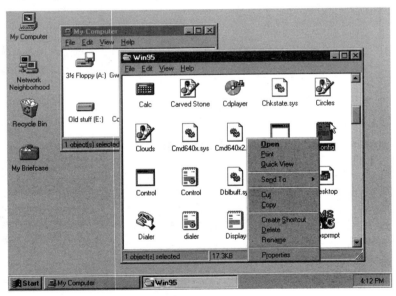

Select Properties from the menu.

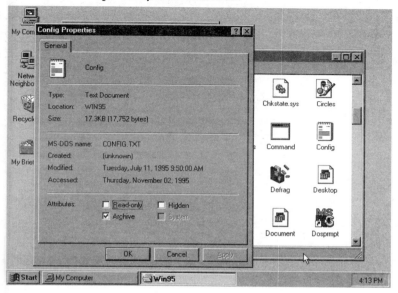

The dialog lists the properties of the document. Some are read/
write and can be changed, for instance, the hidden, archive and
(confusingly) read-only properties of the document; others are
for information only, like the size and date of last modification.

The properties of a folder are similar to those of a document, but
the dialog tells you how many files and folders are contained
within it.

 Close this dialog, then view the properties of a folder.

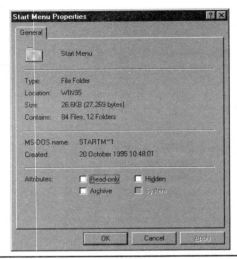

☞ *As you may guess, the contents of the Start Menu folder will appear on the Start Menu. More about the Start Menu later.*

🖑 *View the properties of a disk.*

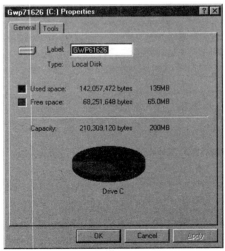

You can see how much space is in use or available on the disk, and view or change the disk's label.

As you can see, the technique for viewing the properties of these objects is the same, even though each object has different properties and does different things. This method of viewing the properties of an object (the Properties option on the context menu) is very common throughout Windows 95.

 In the few instances where it does not work (usually on dialogs), you will find a button to give you access to the properties.

Sometimes, it might not be obvious where to click in order to see the properties of an object. Most of the objects you have seen so far have been represented by convenient icons, but there are some objects that do not have icons on the desktop. How would you view the property sheets for these objects?

One such example is the desktop itself! You have already seen how to change the way in which the desktop appears (colours, wallpaper, screen savers etc.). It is worth while revisiting these in the light of the discussion on properties.

Right-click any blank area of the desktop:

The context menu contains a Properties option. This indicates that Windows 95 views the desktop as an object.

🖱 *Click P<u>r</u>operties...*

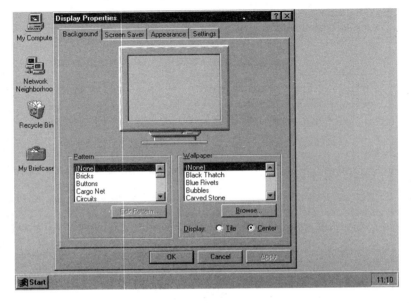

You have seen this dialog before. A point to note here is the
title, Display Properties – from the point of view of Windows 95,
the Desktop properties relate to the way in which the whole of
Windows 95 uses the display.

🖱 *Put away the Display Properties sheet and bring up the
properties sheet for My Computer.*

This dialog displays System Properties. Most of the entries here
are very technical and beyond the scope of this book, so we won't
go into detail here.

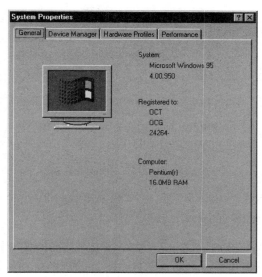

🖰 *Try the properties sheet for the Network Neighborhood.*

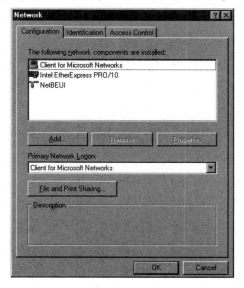

Here we have configuration information about network components (card drivers, clients, services etc. – don't worry about
these for now). Again, the important point is that configuration
information for the network is presented as properties of the
Network Neighborhood, an object that represents the network.

Now, a tricky one; how do you display mouse properties? According to the philosophy we have been expounding so far, you
really ought to right click the graphical representation of the
mouse on the screen. However, you might find right clicking the
mouse pointer a little tricky. There are one or two cases in which
there is no convenient representation on screen of an object whose
properties are important. In order that you can view the properties sheet for such objects, the Control Panel contains icons that
open property sheets directly.

Go to Settings from the Start Menu, click Control Panel:

The Control Panel folder opens.

Most (but not all) of the icons here are property sheets for various objects. Those of you who are familiar with the Control Panel in earlier versions of Windows will recognise that it serves the same purpose — holding configuration information for the whole system. However, now that we have embraced object orientation, you should try to appreciate that the Control Panel fulfils its purpose simply by providing access to the property sheets of important objects.

You can have a look at a few property sheets if you like, but we will not go into a full discussion of each one here.

This selection should not prove at all frightening to try out:

Date/Time   For changing the date and time and time zone information

Display   Actually the same as the desktop properties just mentioned

Fonts   Allows you to examine what fonts are installed, but its real purpose is to allow the installation of new fonts (which might arrive on a floppy disk)

Keyboard	For changing the delay and rate of repeat when you hold down a key, also the language and type (size)
Mouse	Allows you to switch left and right buttons, change pointers and the relative speed of the mouse on the desk and the pointer on screen
Passwords	Allows you to change passwords, but also to decide whether each user has different settings, or all users share the same ones (assuming there are several users of your computer).
Regional	For changing decimal separators, currency symbols, date format and so on
Sounds	If your computer has the capacity to play sounds, you can associate particular sounds with events (like maximizing a window or emptying the bin)

🖰   *Close the Window on to the Control Panel when you have finished.*

Summary: Objects

- Everything in Windows 95 appears as an object.

- Using Ⅴiew, Options... you can choose to move through object contents, e.g. see documents and folders on the C: drive, in a single window, or view each in different windows.

- Every object has properties which can be viewed by selecting Properties from the context menu.

- Certain important objects have an icon in the control panel.

7

THE EXPLORER

This chapter covers:
- Launching the Explorer
- Understanding the Object Hierarchy
- Manipulating Objects
- Using Quick View

Introducing the Explorer

By now you should be familiar with the idea of navigating the hierarchy of objects on your computer using what we may call "standard" windows. Windows 95 provides another method of navigation called the **Explorer.**

The Explorer itself is an application that runs under Windows 95. Several ways exist to run the application, which we will look at later; for the moment, we will use the Taskbar.

Launching the Explorer

The Explorer can be launched from the Start menu:

.. or from a Context Menu

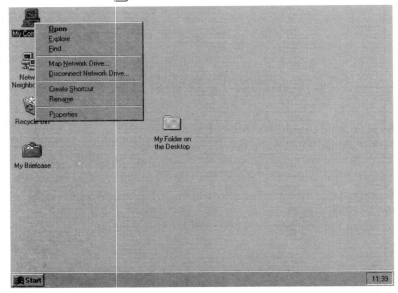

Right-click 🖳 My Computer:

Explorer is also conveniently placed on the context menu of a number of objects – typically those objects that are concerned with files, like the Recycle Bin or My Computer – in which case it will initially display any objects contained in the object concerned.

The default menu item, Open, will display the contents of the My Computer object in a window, but the Explorer gives an alternative approach – in particular, it can provide a view of the **object hierarchy** at the same time as the objects at the current level in the hierarchy:

Choose <u>E</u>xplore from the menu:

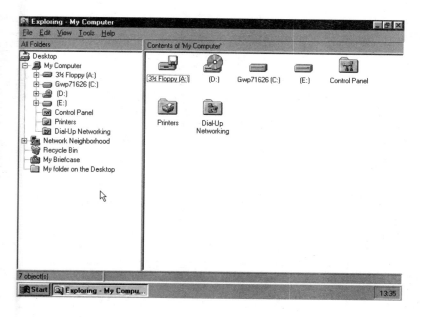

First Impressions

The Purpose of the Explorer

The Explorer allows you to search for and work with certain classes of object – most notably and usefully, folders and files stored on your computer or network drives. It has a hierarchical structure of objects you can access, with the highest level being the desktop.

>   *Users of earlier versions of windows might be amused to know that some people involved in the development of Windows 95 were known to refer to the Explorer as 'the File Manager on steroids'!*

The window is split into two panes. In the left-hand pane are displayed all the container objects within their hierarchy; the contents of the currently selected one are displayed in the right-hand pane (the contents of 'My Computer' in this case, as that is the object you right-clicked, and whose context menu you used).

Windows Settings

The Explorer is, in a sense, just another window – certainly the options for viewing the objects in the right-hand pane are similar to those you have already seen in an earlier chapter for a window, and the current options are remembered from the last session of using the Explorer. So what you see may differ considerably from the above. If you wish your window to match ours, you may need to use the View menu, and to maximise the window.

Finding Your Way Around

The first object that you see in Windows 95 is the desktop, and this is at the top of the hierarchy.

You should find that the desktop contains all the folders that you have on your desktop plus the 🖳 My Computer object, the 🖳 Network Neighborhood object and the 🗑 Recycle Bin.

The representation of the object hierarchy is intended to represent levels of containment (which you might think of as levels of importance). The desktop contains everything, including anything on your company network, or any other networks you can access. You probably spend most time working with objects on your computer. Although your computer could be considered to be in the network, it is far more important to you than everyone else's machine. Therefore 🖳 My Computer appears as an object at the same level within the desktop as the whole network. When you view the 🖳 Network Neighborhood you will find that the other computers in your workgroup appear before the Entire Network for the same reason.

Expanding and Collapsing the Hierarchy

Next to some of the objects in the left pane you will see either a ⊞ or a ⊟ symbol. Clicking ⊞ will expand the contents of an object (and the ⊞ is replaced by a ⊟); clicking ⊟ will collapse the view of the contents (and the ⊟ is replaced by a ⊞). If neither appears next to an object, the hierarchy finishes there – the object concerned contains no other object container.

For example, in our case, My Computer contains a number of drives; each drive might contain a number of folders. Consider drive C: (labelled Gwp71626 – yours will be different). It sports a ⊞ to indicate that there are folders within it, currently not shown.

 Carefully click the ⊞ next to a hard drive.

If you clicked it accurately, you will now be looking at the next level of the hierarchy within this drive:

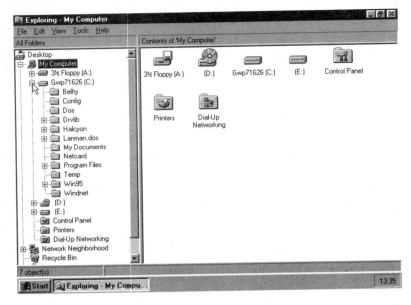

It now sports a ⊟ to remind you that you can collapse this branch of the hierarchy again. Looking at the objects now revealed within this drive, you can see that some sport a ⊞ (indicating that they contain folders), and some do not (indicating that they contain only files, or perhaps nothing at all).

Note that the right-hand pane of the window still shows the contents of 'My Computer'.

Selecting an Object

If you had clicked the icon or name of the object (perhaps intending to hit the ⊞, but missing), you would have selected the object, and the right-hand pane would show the objects in this container object:

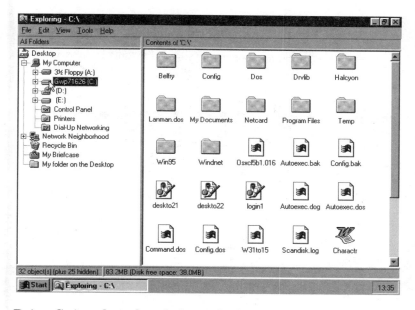

Drive C: is selected and the right-hand pane shows you the objects (files and folders) in that drive – i.e. the next level of the hierarchy (of course they in turn may hold other objects, and so on). Note, though, that the hierarchy would not have been expanded (as in the case of clicking the ⊞).

Had you double-clicked the object, you would have opened it. In this context that means both expanding the hierarchy and selecting the object. Double-clicking an object that is sporting a ⊟ both collapses that branch of the hierarchy and selects the object.

You will have noticed that some objects appear both in the left- and right-hand panes – double-clicking a folder in the right-hand pane has much the same effect as double-clicking it on the left – it opens it. But watch out, because double-clicking a file (i.e. opening it) has a different effect – it opens that file in another window, if it can.

Renaming an Object

If you first select an object, and then click its name (not too quickly, or it is interpreted as a double-click), it may respond by allowing you to edit its name (depending on what kind of object it is):

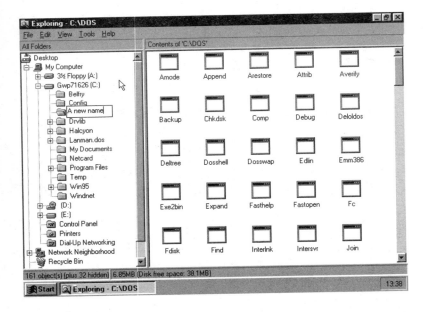

Practice

You will need to experiment for a while with the use of the hierarchy in the left-hand pane, starting to get used to clicking the objects themselves, the ⊞ and ⊟ markers and double-clicking the objects.

🖱 *Continuing our example, click the* ⊞ *next to the Win95 folder, to expand it:*

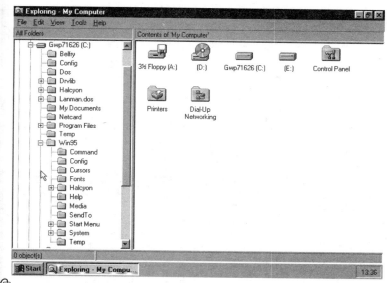

Click the Win95 folder to select it:

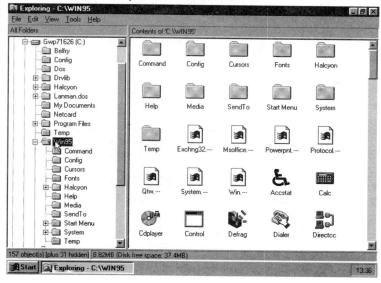

The right-hand pane now shows the contents of 'C:\Win95' (rather than 'My Computer').

Some View Options

As already mentioned, there are many options for how you view the objects in the right-hand pane – some examples follow:

Click the *View* menu and select *Small Icons:*

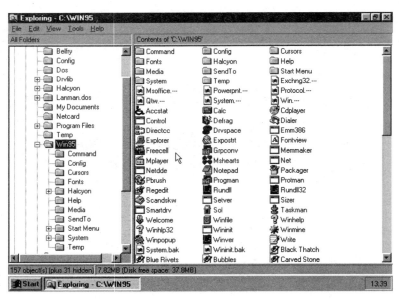

You could have done this by right-clicking the background of the right-hand pane and using the context menu.

Click the *View* menu and select *List:*

Click the <u>V</u>iew menu and select <u>D</u>etails:

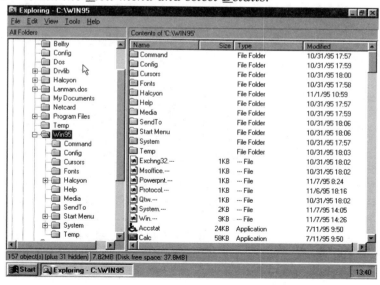

The Toolbar

 Click the View menu and select Toolbar (assuming this was not already switched on):

Here is what the buttons do:

'Up one level' – when you click this, you move up through the hierarchy of container objects, i.e. you select whichever object contains the object which is currently selected in the left-hand pane. For example, if the C: drive was selected, clicking would select My Computer. The right-hand pane will change to display the contents of the newly selected container object. This does not really do anything that you couldn't do using the hierarchical display on the left, but it can be convenient, and it appears in other windows that do not display the hierarchy.

[icon] and [icon] Respectively map (connect) and disconnect a network drive. These are covered in a later chapter.

[icon] [icon] and [icon] Cut, copy and paste – these can be used to copy and move of files and folders.

[icon] Undo – undoes the last action, if possible.

[icon] *Take care – not every action can be undone (e.g. deleting a file on a mapped network drive).*

[icon] Delete the selected object(s) – be careful! The delete key ([Delete]) can also delete.

[icon] Properties – you can examine/edit object properties, as explained earlier.

[icon] [icon] [icon] and [icon] These correspond to the View options Large Icons, Small Icons, List and Detail.

All of these can be done through the window and/or context menus – the tools are a further convenience.

Go To a Different Folder

At the left end of the toolbar, there is a 'Go To a Different Folder' drop down, which displays a subset of the hierarchy – the immediate context of the currently selected object and all the 'important' objects, like drives. This is often the most convenient way of navigating, particularly when you want to take a 'large jump', for instance to another drive or computer.

Other Explorer Features

There are other features, but here we are only trying to introduce the Explorer. Other View options, standard on many windows, have already been covered in earlier chapters.

The Explorer can be used to search for files anywhere from the desktop level down. The find utility is covered in a later chapter.

This chapter continues by describing some typical usages of the Explorer – this will give you a further opportunity to practise what you have done so far.

☝ *Remember that there are many settings you can change, many of which are kept for future sessions – so don't be surprised if your screen doesn't look like ours.*

You will find that if you open a new Explorer session when you already have one going, it may not use the same settings, and that when you close them again, settings are not always 'remembered' as you might expect.

———— Object Manipulation ————

The Explorer can be used to move and copy files/documents with left-click and right-click dragging methods, as well as through the cut, copy and paste features. Files/documents can have their properties modified, be deleted (e.g. by pressing [Delete]) or be opened (by double-clicking their icon). Right-clicking a document will still display its context menu, giving you the full list of options.

Scroll down the Explorer window until you can see the icon for your folder on the desktop in the list on the left.

Click the icon for this folder.

The right side of the Explorer window now shows what is in the folder. The icon for the text document should be displayed. You could open the document from the explorer by double-clicking its icon.

 Instead, right-click the document icon.

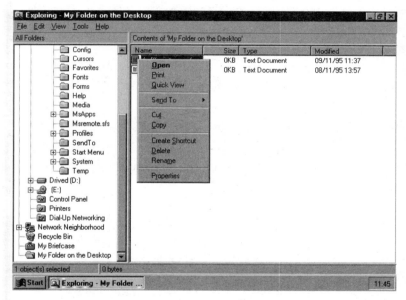

From here you could choose to open the document, print it, delete it, view its properties – indeed many different actions can be taken.

The Explorer is very useful for manipulating objects. As an example, you will move this folder from the desktop on to the C: drive, then rename it (see the next chapter for guidance on how to organise your files and folders).

Moving and Copying Objects

Moving, and copying, objects in the Explorer can most readily be done by dragging an object from its original location and dropping it into its new one.

As explained in an earlier chapter, if you drag an object (with the left mouse button) between locations on the same drive, the default is to move, but holding down ⌈Ctrl⌉ forces a copy; dragging an object between drives defaults to a copy, but holding down ⌈Shift⌉ forces a move. Dragging with the right mouse button does the same, except that when you drop the object, a menu appears allowing you to decide to make it a move, a copy, to create a shortcut (see a later chapter) or to cancel the operation altogether.

👍 *Remember that if you made a mistake, you will usually be able to undo it using* ↩

As an exercise you are going to move your desktop folder ('My folder on the desktop') into drive C: – the trick is to make sure you can see both, facilitating the drag operation.

🖱 *In the left-hand pane, scroll right to the top so that you can see both the Desktop icon and the Drive C: icon.*

Click the Desktop icon.

All folders on the desktop should now be displayed in the right-hand pane.

🖱 *Drag the folder from the right-hand pane (from the desk-top list) and drop it on to the C: drive icon in the left-hand pane.*

The folder disappears from the Desktop list and reappears in the list for the C: drive (it will eventually move into its correct alphabetical position):

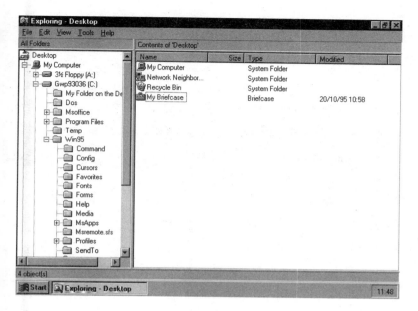

By the way, the folder icon will no longer appear on the desktop itself, either.

The above instruction is a fine example of something that is really quite simple and intuitive appearing complicated when written down. In general you can drag an object from anywhere you can see it, to anywhere that makes sense.

So we could have dragged the desktop folder from the desktop itself into the Explorer, and vice-versa. A folder can be dragged between two places in the hierarchical display in the left-hand pane, or from the left-hand pane to the right-hand pane.

As you drag, a ⊞ symbol will appear if the default is to copy (and will appear and disappear to reflect the fact that you might hold down Ctrl or Shift). A 'no waiting' symbol indicates that you may not drop the object at this point (if you try, the operation is simply cancelled).

As you can see, the Explorer makes transferring files or folders from one location to another very simple.

You could now rename the folder.

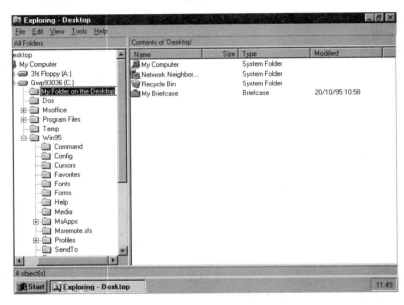

Right-click the icon for your folder in the C: drive list and choose Rename – or simply click the name.

The icon title becomes highlighted and you can rename the folder.

Type in a new name for the folder, e.g. My Documents.

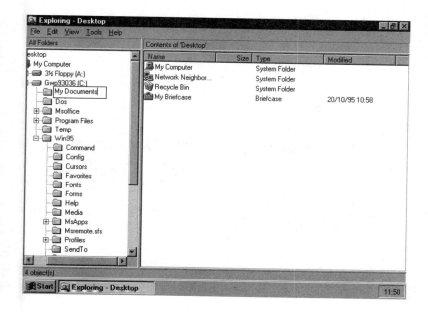

Using Quick View

This is an extremely useful Windows 95 utility that presents you with a **quick view** of a file – i.e. without having to load the application that would normally be associated with it. This doesn't work for all files, only 'well-known' ones. So it works for Word documents, Excel worksheets, Powerpoint slideshows and so on (though it is only a 'rough look'); but not for a compressed archive file, for example.

> Quick View does not work for all files, and does not present all the features of more complex files (that is the job of the originating application) – but it is usually more than good enough to be able to see what the file is about.

If you like the look of the file, you can open the file from the Quick View window.

🖰 *Click the Win95 folder icon.*

The folders and files contained here are now displayed.

🖰 *Locate the* CLOUDS *bitmap file and right-click its icon.*

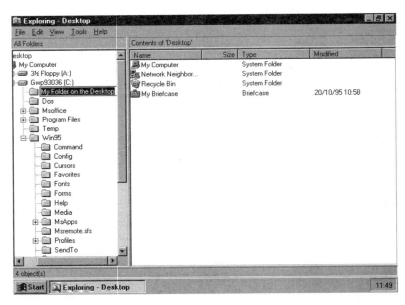

🖰 *Choose Quick View.*

If the file type was not one that can be Quick Viewed, the option would not appear in the context menu.

A window opens, displaying the picture.

Quick View allows you to view the contents of the file, but is intended to do little else. If you have an application which can open the document, you can select the File menu in Quick View and choose to Open the File for Editing.

Close down any windows you have opened in this chapter (e.g. the Quick View and Explorer windows).

Summary: The Explorer

- The Windows 95 Explorer displays any objects which you have access to.

- The left-hand pane displays a representation of the object hierarchy, while the right-hand pane displays the objects contained in the currently selected container object.

- The highest level in the hierarchy is the desktop, which will contain 🖳 My Computer, the 🖳 Network Neighborhood and the 🗑 Recycle Bin at least.

- The Explorer is very useful for locating, opening, copying and moving files.

- Quick View allows you to display the contents of a file on screen prior to opening, deleting, copying etc.

- Usually there are several ways of activating a feature menu, context menu or toolbar - choose whichever is most convenient.

- Settings are generally remembered from one session to the next.

8

───────── STORAGE ─────────

This chapter covers:
- Storing documents on the desktop
- Creating and using shortcuts
- Some guidance on where to store your date

Storing documents on the Desktop

Any file (document) or folder can be stored on the desktop. The analogy with a real desktop would be that you were keeping your documents on the desk rather than filing them away. This is, of course, precisely the way that people work. The documents that you are using most often are kept closest to hand, less frequently used ones are filed.

It is not a good idea to store too many files on your desktop as it can get very cluttered. You will probably find that the desktop makes a useful temporary storage space, especially if you are moving a document between two folders when it is difficult to drag directly from one folder to the other.

It is possible to configure Windows 95 so that when each user logs on they get their own desktop. Therefore documents that you have stored on your desktop will not appear on the desktops of other people.

 Documents stored on the desktop are actually stored on disk in a hidden folder, C:\WINDOWS\DESKTOP

Shortcuts

One way of moving quickly to an object (e.g. a file or folder) that has already been stored away somewhere else is to create a **shortcut** to it. A shortcut is itself an object – actually a file with the extension .LNK. Shortcuts have two important advantages: the shortcut files stored on your computer are quite small, and when you open a shortcut it is the object to which the shortcut points that is actually opened.

Shortcuts can be stored anywhere that can contain file objects, but are often stored on the desktop, or in a folder on the desktop. Shortcuts can be made to computers, drives etc. – but perhaps most often to files (documents) and folders.

 Another important use of shortcuts is in the Start menu. For instance the Programs part of the Start menu is made up out of shortcuts (to the programs themselves), and the organisation of these shortcuts defines the layout of the menu system. The actual shortcuts are stored in the Startup folder in the Windows folder.

Document Shortcuts

In the context of the above discussion, a document shortcut on the desktop is like a button on your desk, which, when you press it, retrieves the document from your filing system – immediately and without all that tedious searching through your filing cabinet. But the file itself still resides in the filing cabinet so that everyone knows where it is really kept. You have the convenience of quick access via your desktop, without people accusing you of leaving important files lying around!

Example

First of all you will need a document to make a shortcut to.

Either using Explorer or by opening 🖳 *My Computer, find the Paint picture* **Circles** *in the* **windows** *folder.*

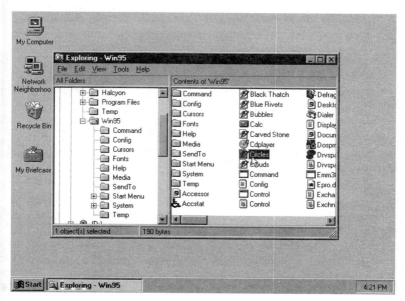

👍 *The Windows folder could be called anything, depending on how it was installed — Win95 and Windows are typical examples.*

🖱️ *With your right mouse button, drag this file on to the desktop.*

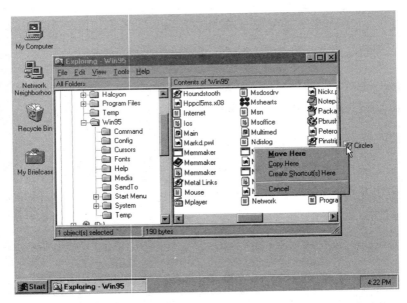

You will remember that when you drop a file with the right mouse button, a context menu appears. As well as the choices to move or copy, there is also the option to Create Shortcut(s).

👍 *If you used the left button by mistake, you have simply moved the file — this can be undone (↶) or moved (dragged) back again.*

Choose Create Shortcut(s) Here.

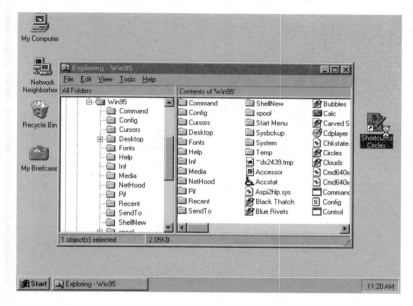

Windows 95 creates a document on the desktop called Shortcut
to Circles. Notice the ▣ in the corner of the icon to indicate that
it is a shortcut. If you right-click the shortcut you should see
that it has the same context menu as the original document. If
you Open the shortcut, Windows 95 will open the original document – but the shortcut is not a copy.

 *Open the shortcut (using the context menu or by double-
clicking).*

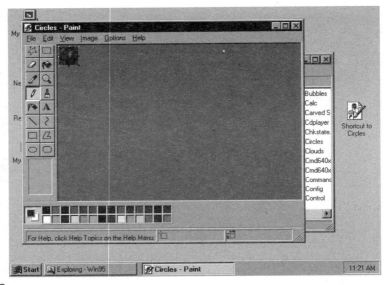

🖱 *Edit the picture and save the changes.*

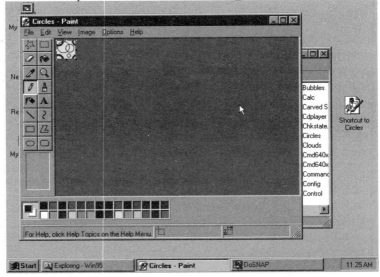

If the shortcut was really only a copy of the document, the changes you made would only be saved in the shortcut and not in the original document.

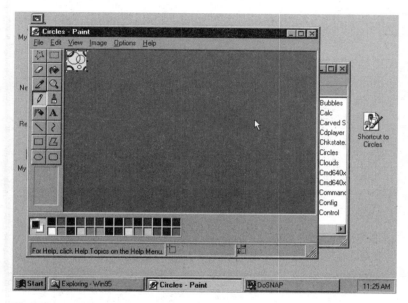

Close Paint and open the original document (not the shortcut).

The changes you made have been saved in the original document.

You can create shortcuts to any object including programs, disk drives, printers, even the 🗑 Recycle Bin. Shortcuts do not have to be on the desktop either. You can add them anywhere where you are allowed to store a file, where they will serve as navigation aids.

Application shortcuts

Another way to create a shortcut is to use the Create Shortcut wizard. This time you will create a shortcut to an application program. Shortcuts such as these can be very useful because they provide another easy way to launch applications in addition to the Start menu.

🖱 *Right-click the desktop and choose New from the menu.*

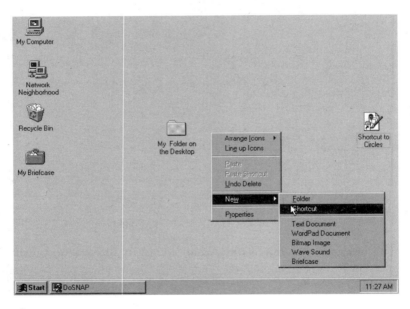

🖱 *From the New menu choose Shortcut.*

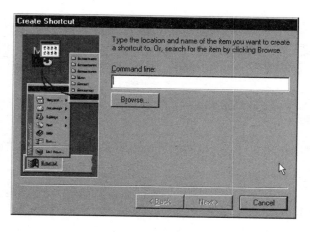

This is the Create Shortcut wizard. In the box labelled 'Command line:' the wizard is expecting the name and path of a program, document or folder. You can use shortcuts to start programs with special switches. This is similar to creating icons in Program Manager in Windows 3.x. You will find that you do not normally need to add to the command line of Windows programs in Windows 95 but you may still need to do this with MS-DOS applications.

If you are unsure of the name or location of the file, you can click Browse... *to locate it.*

Create a shortcut to Notepad, which can usually be found in the Windows directory.

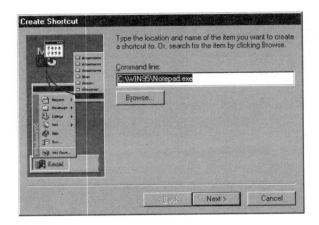

🖰 *Click* Next >

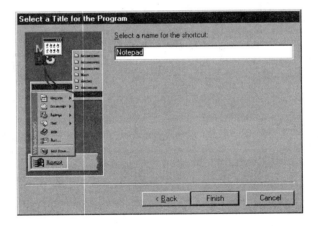

🖰 *Enter a title (name) for the shortcut if you like (it doesn't have to say 'Notepad') and click* Finish

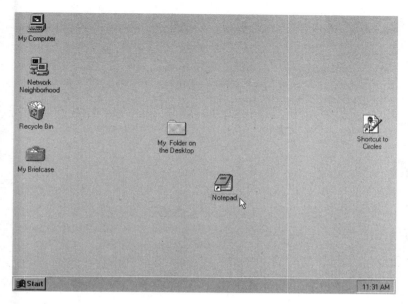

Opening this shortcut will launch Notepad.

   Try it.

——— Where to Store Your Data ———

In this section we attempt to give some guidelines on where to store your data. Data is stored in document files – other files might hold programs – but the terms 'file' and 'document' tend to be used interchangeably. A slight confusion is brought about when referring to documents, because (for instance) a Word Document is a type of document (file), but an Excel Worksheet is also a type of document (file). The term 'document' should be understood to mean any collection of data that you are working on with any application (stored as a file in your filing system).

– 149 –

Hierarchy

In the chapter on the Explorer, it started to become clear that
there is a hierarchy of Windows objects. An understanding of
this hierarchy is key to effective organisation of your data. You
may remember that the hierarchy starts from your desktop. The
next layer is 'anything on your desktop' – My Computer, Network
Neighborhood, Recycle Bin, any folders you have added to the
desktop etc. Within My Computer, and any computers you come
across on the Network, you find drives and then folders. Within
the folders you find files (documents, programs etc.)

An Analogy

In terms of a filing system, a useful analogy might be that computers are equivalent to filing cabinets, drives like drawers in
those cabinets and top-level folders are the hanging files in those
drawers. The folders may contain more folders, and so on. Ulti-
mately our folders contain files.

Conventions

In a manual filing system there are some obvious DOs and
DONTs, some well-understood conventions (because they seem
obvious, or because a company imposes them), and some rather
less well-understood ones. And there are different conventions
used in different organisations – many just as good as each other,
some not very good – but the worst scenario is no convention at
all!

Guidelines

We won't try to come up with any rules here – but we can suggest some guidelines. For instance, you will find you can store
documents directly in a drive, not in any folder (sometimes called
the 'root' of the drive) and this is equivalent to storing files in
the bottom of a filing cabinet drawer – we can say don't do it,
but we can point out that it is untidy. Actually floppy disks

represent a reasonable exception to this 'rule', because they are so small that organisation of the data on them is not usually a problem.

Files and Folders

A warning about long names

Be careful when you use long names. Windows 95 and Windows NT machines will be able to read the long names that you have created, but machines that are still running MS-DOS and Windows 3.x will not see the long names.

These other machines will still see the files and folders but they will appear with 8.3 character names instead (8 characters then a dot then 3 characters). These names are generated by Windows 95. For instance a text document called NEW TEXT DOCU-MENT will appear to MS-DOS users as NEWTEX~1.TXT The number after the ~ is incremented to avoid duplicating the names.

> *It is possible to configure Windows 95 so that the ~ is not used in the generated short filenames. If this is so the short filenames are constructed by removing any unsupported characters, such as spaces, then taking the first eight characters of the long filename. So in the example above, the short filename would be* NEWTEXTD.TXT. *This will happen as long as the resulting short filename is not the same as that for an existing file.*

If you never imagine using an operating system other than Windows 95 or Windows NT, then you can probably name your files freely. If you are working in a mixed environment, then at the very least you should take a little care when naming files. You might even consider sticking with an 8.3 regime until you understand the consequences, or you find that the majority of time is spent in the new operating systems.

Folders

Even on a floppy disk, it makes sense to create at least one folder (rather than copy all your files into the disk itself), and if you have a lot of files, to create several folders at several levels grouping your files by type, or by an association to a particular client of project.

If you look at your principle hard drive (very likely drive C:), you will find that Windows itself has put some special files in the drive itself (i.e. not in any folder) we suggest you do not add to these and that you certainly don't delete them!

A common (and sensible) way to group data, and hence to build up a folder structure is to create some high level directories which divide into my data, someone else's data, programs of a general kind, a certain set of programs (like MS Office) and so on.

For instance Microsoft Office, left to it own devices, might create a top level directory in drive C: called MSOffice, underneath which you will find folders called Excel, Powerpnt and Winword (amongst others) each of these has a whole structure of folders underneath it pertaining to the particular application (Excel, Powerpoint or Word for Windows). Anything they need in common (like Clip Art) will be put in a suitably named folder just within MSOffice.

In the same way, you might create a folder called 'MyStuff' under which you create further folders to group your data by file type (Figure 8.1), or you might group your data by who or what the data refers to, putting any type of file (picture, worksheet etc.) into the same folder. (Figure 8.2).

And many other arrangements will work just as well.

Arrange the structure so that files are reasonably well spread (not all in one folder with the others mostly empty) but don't get hung up on that idea, you'll rarely get them very even. Too few folders means too many files in each folder; and too many folders means ages hunting around for a folder that only con-

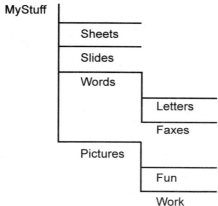

Figure 8.1

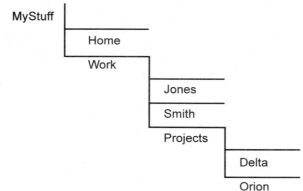

Figure 8.2

tains a few files. Also, too few files at any level means more levels underneath; but too many means it is harder to get a clear view at that level.

File Naming Conventions

Again, any convention is better than no convention at all. Just calling file doc1, letter3 etc. is unlikely to facilitate quick and efficient retrieval later on.

If you are restricting yourself to an 8.3 regime, then you might consider the following guidelines useful:

- Generally try to use the 3 character extension to define only the type, keeping the 8 letter name unique.

- Come to some sort of agreement about the use of the 8 letter name.

- You don't usually need to include date information, because the data and time of last modification is stored anyway although you sometime need to indicate which month or year a report (for instance) relates to (like Sales95.xls, or Cost9612.xls – meaning December 1996).

- If you have a well-structured hierarchy of folders, naming is less of a problem. For instance, if you are organising a small number of documents with a folder for each client you are dealing with, letter01, letter02 might really be enough.

- Where you have a lot of files in one folder, you might consider a convention that uses a short code to represent the company name, followed by the initials of the recipient and then a number (e.g. OCG_HW01.doc meaning the first letter written to someone with the initials HW at a company known as OCG. If you do this, it is good to use a standard number of characters for each element of the name (here we used 'OCG_', making it up to 4 characters) this will facilitate searching later on (in this case files of type ????HW??.* could readily be searched for, knowing that the HW will always occupy the 5th and 6th position, whether the company was OCG, BT or BICC.

If you are going to use long names – and everyone will do eventually – you can be a bit more relaxed, but people with the discipline to use a shortish name efficiently will always be able to access those old files more quickly than those who use long, rambling ones.

In the end, all we can suggest is that you sit down with any other interested parties and think of some sort of convention **before** you get too far down the road!

Summary: Storage

- Documents can be stored on the desktop as well as in folders.

- You can create shortcuts to documents and folders to make files easier to find.

- Long document names are not visible to users of Windows 3.x and MS-DOS, but the files can be used with an automatically generated short name.

- It is worthwhile thinking about where you will store data and coming up with some kind of convention.

9

—THE RECYCLE BIN—

This chapter covers:

- Sending documents to the 🗑 Recycle Bin and recovering them
- Emptying the 🗑 Recycle Bin
- Configuring the 🗑 Recycle Bin

—— What is the Recycle Bin? ——

When documents are deleted in Windows 95, they are not necessarily removed from the system immediately. Windows 95 allocates a portion of your disk to use as a 🗑 Recycle Bin where it stores the documents that you delete. The analogy is with an office rubbish bin, but one from which you can retrieve or 'recycle' files and folders (and the name is nicely in tune with the 'green' spirit of the time).

Unlike your real office bin, it is possible to configure the exact size of the 🗑 Recycle Bin area. Like the real bin, however, you will be able to recover documents that you have thrown away in error, remembering of course that once the Bin has been emptied the document can no longer be retrieved.

The bin in your office may well be emptied daily (after which a trip to the rubbish dump is the only hope of retrieval). The Recycle Bin is usually emptied only when you say (it is not automatically emptied at Shutdown), though when there is not enough allocated space left for a deleted document to be stored, some of the documents in the Bin will be removed to make space.

Sending documents to the Recycle Bin

You can send a document to the Recycle Bin by deleting it.

Select Shortcut to Circles and press Delete

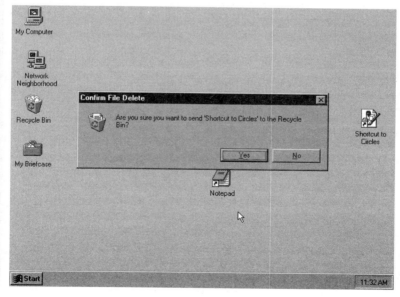

You are asked to confirm the action. You would see the same result if you chose **Delete** from the context menu:

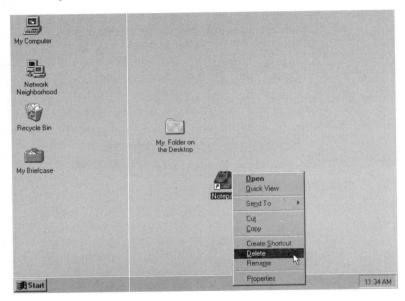

Often, the easiest way to send something to the 🗑 Recycle Bin is to drag and drop it there. When you do this you will not be asked to confirm the action.

Recovering files from the Recycle Bin

Examining Deleted Files

The files that you have deleted most recently will still be in the 🗑 Recycle Bin. Opening the 🗑 Recycle Bin will display them.

Open the  *Recycle Bin.*

The exact appearance of the 🗑 Recycle Bin window depends on settings in the View menu. The view options are similar to those of the windows we have looked at before, including the availability of a toolbar.

 Double-click a document in the 🗑 *Recycle Bin folder.*

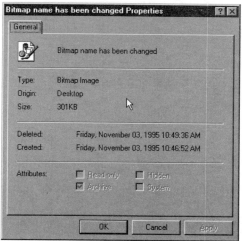

☝ *You cannot edit a document when it is in the* 🗑*Recycle Bin. You must restore it first.*

The default action for an object in the 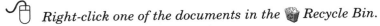 Recycle Bin is not to open it but to display its properties. If you have several copies of the same document in the Recycle Bin, you can double-click each of them to find out which of the files you intend to restore (perhaps using the Deleted date as the criterion).

Restoring Files

 Right-click one of the documents in the Recycle Bin.

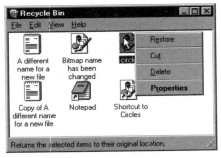

If you choose restore from this menu it will return the document to the folder from which you deleted it.

Try restoring a document using the menu.

Restoring by Dragging

You can restore a document from the Recycle Bin by dragging it back out of the Bin on to the desktop or into a folder.

Try restoring a document by dragging it on to the desktop.

So you can also restore a file 'to somewhere else' by dragging it from the Recycle Bin to another location (Desktop, folder etc.)

– you may recognise that this is not exactly restoring it, but it is nevertheless useful to be able to put a deleted file somewhere else entirely.

A file can only be moved by this method, never copied.

———— Emptying the Recycle Bin ————

If you are sure that you no longer need the documents that are in the 🗑 Recycle Bin you can delete them individually by selecting them in the 🗑 Recycle Bin folder window and pressing

🖱 *Select a document from the bin and press* ⌨Delete

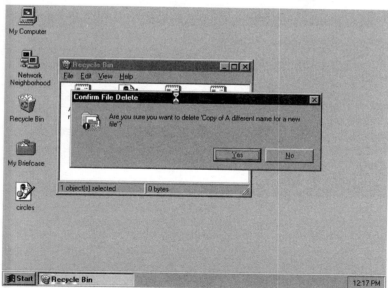

Once a document has been deleted from the Bin it cannot be retrieved!

✍ *There are a number of utilities available for DOS and Windows 3.x which try to recover files from your hard disk even after you have deleted them. Because Windows 95 controls the hard disk in a different way from these older systems, it is quite likely that such utilities will not work in Windows 95.*

If you want to delete all of the files in the Bin then you can do this using the context menu.

🖱 *Right-click the 🗑 Recycle Bin.*

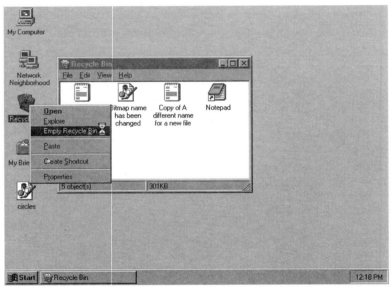

When you select Empty Recycle Bin from the menu ALL of the files in the Bin will be PERMANENTLY deleted.

🖱 *Select Empty Recycle Bin from the menu.*

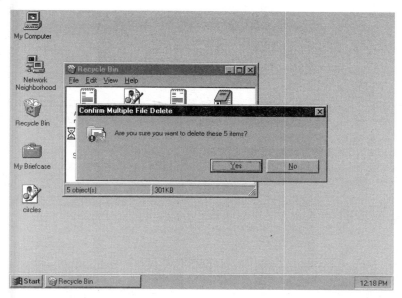

Multiple deletions can be made by holding down Ctrl while you click on objects. This allows you to select only those items you are sure about – you then press Delete to complete the procedure.

—— Configuring the Recycle Bin ——

It is possible to change how much space is allocated for storing deleted documents. This is done by changing the properties of the Recycle Bin.

 Right-click the 🗑 *Recycle Bin (or the background area of its window) and choose Properties...*

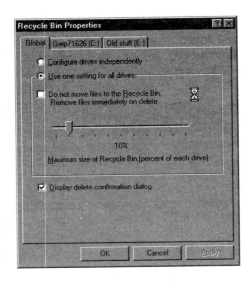

The Recycle Bin allocates space on all your fixed disk drives. The amount of space allocated to the Recycle Bin is a percentage of your original disk space. The default setting is 10%. You can configure different amounts on each drive if you wish.

Be careful to monitor the contents of the Recycle Bin. If the Bin becomes full (i.e. it exceeds the Maximum size allocated in the Properties dialog) the files which have been in it longest will be deleted to make room for later disposals. The files are deleted without a warning dialog to inform you what is happening.

Try dragging to change the amount of space allocated.

If you select ☑ 'Do not move files to the Recycle Bin' then they will be deleted without being placed in the Recycle Bin. You will not be able to recover ANY files that you have deleted. If you have not got much free disk space then this setting may be necessary.

Notice that you can also switch off the delete confirmation message boxes from the Recycle Bin Properties dialog.

 Close the window when you have finished experimenting.

—— Files which cannot be recycled ——

Not every file you work with can be restored once you have
dragged it to the 🗑 Recycle Bin or chosen to <u>D</u>elete it from its
context menu. In such cases there is no way to recover the file
once you have clicked to confirm the deletion. To prevent acci-
dental, but permanent, loss of such files it is worth briefly con-
sidering some basic guidelines.

You saw in the previous section that the 🗑 Recycle Bin can be
configured to use a certain amount of space on each of your
computer's fixed disk drives. If the file you are deleting is too
big to fit in the 🗑 Recycle Bin area, it is deleted from the disk
straight away, without going into the Bin first.

Another situation in which a file will be instantly deleted rather
than put into the 🗑 Recycle Bin is when the file is not stored on
one of the hard disks of your computer. This is true for files on a
floppy disk (typically the A: drive) or on a hard disk on someone
else's computer in your 🖳 Network Neighborhood (see the next
chapter for more discussion of the 🖳 Network Neighborhood).

Summary: The Recycle Bin

- Deleted files are normally moved to the 🗑 Recycle Bin.

- Files can be recovered by dragging them out of the 🗑 Recycle Bin.

- Files can be returned to the place they were deleted from by selecting Restore from the context menu.

- The space required for the 🗑 Recycle Bin is configured by changing its properties.

- Some files will be deleted instantly with no option to restore them from the 🗑 Recycle Bin.

10

THE NETWORK NEIGHBORHOOD

This chapter covers:
- Connecting to other computers on the network
- Sharing folders
- Using network resources

Networks

The topic of networks is a tricky one to cover in a book of this nature. Networks come in so many varieties that it would be impossible to cover every situation.

Networks range in size from two simple workstations connected together in the same office by a piece of cable, to many thousands of different types of machine located all over the world and connected by many different means. There are hundreds (possibly thousands) of separate software components that may be used in a single network. Dozens of operating systems are available, hundreds of versions of network software, thousands of makes and models of workstation.

In short, we must concentrate on those features of a network that are likely to be common to the majority of networks and of most interest to the average user (if there is such a thing) of Windows 95.

Having said that, there is one distinction that you may well come across quite frequently; the difference between a **workgroup** and a **client-server** network.

Workgroups

One feature that the vast majority of networks have in common is the ability to allow others to access files, folders and printers on your machine. The corollary being that you can access these **resources** (as they are known) on other people's machines. In the case of a workgroup, all the machines that participate are of similar specification (processor type, amount of memory and disk space etc.). They all tend to have roughly the same amount of resources available and contribute them to the network. Therefore, the machines tend to spend some time allowing other machines access to resources, and some time accessing resources on other machines. Such an arrangement is often known as **peer-to-peer** networking, no computer can be singled out as being 'more important' than any other.

In some circumstances, the user finds themselves in the role of network administrator; deciding which resources to make available and what security (passwords) should be applied. In other circumstances they are the **client** on the network; they request certain resources and are granted use of them by, typically, being supplied with the name and password for that resource.

Client-Server

The workgroup environment described above works very well in some circumstances. However, certainly for larger groups of users, workgroups can become very difficult to administer. Client-Server arrangements address this problem.

In a Client-Server environment, resources and administration are centralised. The network would tend to consist of a small number of large, powerful computers (known as **servers**) that hold the majority of resources. The resources are accessed and used by a larger number of **clients** or workstations, which are usually computers of lower specification than the servers.

Administration is centralised by holding a list of usernames and passwords on the servers. Anyone who wishes to access any resources on any of the network servers must first supply a correct (existing) username and the corresponding password. This process is generally known (not always correctly) as **logging on**. There is usually one (or more) network administrator who is responsible for setting security on resources, maintaining user accounts, setting rules on those accounts and generally enabling the users of the network to get on with useful work.

 漯 *Network Administrators are useful people to know, especially if things are going wrong.*

At the start of the book we discussed the concept of logging on in enough detail to get you past the initial logon dialog of Windows 95. If you work on a networked machine, it is probably worth while finding what general type of network you are attached to and exactly how the logon process works for your particular 'brand' of network.

Sharing resources
on the network

The process of making resources on your machine available for others to use is known as sharing. Sharing is an easy process (as you will soon discover) but Windows 95 must have the correct components installed to allow sharing to happen.

🖰 *Right-click the 🖳 Network Neighborhood icon (or whatever you have renamed it) and choose Properties...*

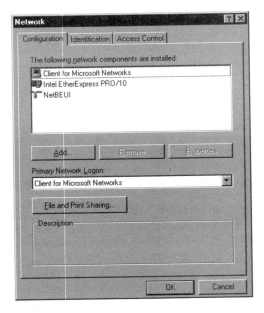

This is the Network properties dialog that you have seen before. This is not the place for a detailed discussion of all options; the one of interest is File and Print Sharing.

Click the File and Print Sharing button...

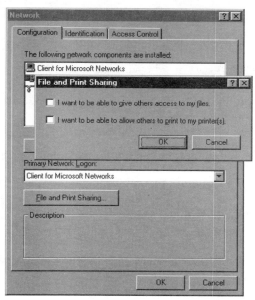

If the checkboxes are unchecked you need to check them now.

Check the checkboxes if necessary, then click OK *and* OK *again to close the Network properties dialog.*

> What you have asked Windows 95 to do is to install something called File and Print Sharing Services. If these were not installed before, you may find that you need to supply Windows 95 with the installation files for your machine. If you are working in a large network and Windows 95 was installed for you, you may have to contact your network administrator at this point.

After changing your network configuration settings, you often need to restart your computer to make them take effect. If this is the case you will be informed with a dialog:

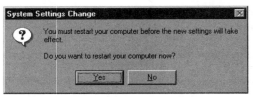

🖰 *If you see this dialog, click and wait for your computer and Windows 95 to restart.*

Assuming the installation has worked, we will continue (if it hasn't, then you will need to seek help).

Sharing Folders

We will use folders as the main example of resource sharing.

🖰 *Open a window on the C: drive in* 🖳 *My Computer.*

All folders which permit sharing will have a Sharing... option on their context menu.

🖱 *Right-click a folder and choose Sharing... from the context menu.*

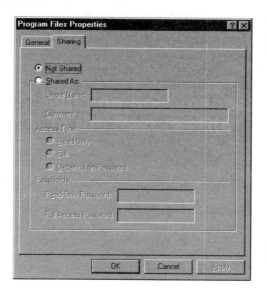

The options will allow you to share this folder.

🖱 *Click ⊙ Shared As.*

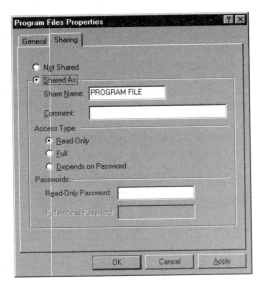

The share name is the name this folder will have when it is viewed by other computers. You can also add a comment to give some information about what is in the folder (for example, 'Monthly Sales Sheets').

If you share the folder Read-Only, the other users will be able to read the files and run the programs in the share but they will not be able to change them, delete them or add more files to the folder.

If the Access Type is Full then the other users will be able to use the folder in exactly the same way that they use their own folders. They will be able to add, delete and edit all the files in the folder.

For both of these actions, it is possible to add a password so that users connecting over the network will not be able to see your files if they do not have the password. If you select Depends on Password as the Access type then they will be asked for a password when they try to open the folder and will be given the level of access which matches the password they have typed (you should use different passwords for each access type for this to work). If their password does not match either of the access passwords then they will not be able to see your files at all.

🖱 *Share your folder as* **Test** *and set the Access Type to Read-Only. Set the Password to* **Password**

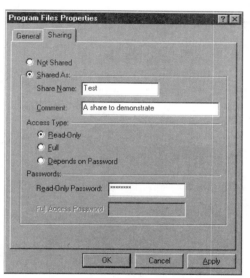

🖱 *Click* [OK]

To be sure that you have not accidentally mis-typed your password you are asked to type it in again.

Folders on your computer which you have shared will have a different icon to non-shared folders; a hand appears beneath the folder: 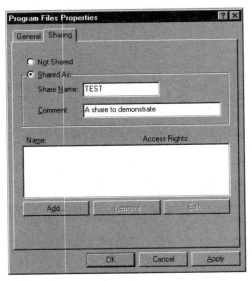 If circumstances permit, you might like to arrange for a friend or colleague who also has a Windows 95 computer to attempt to connect to your share.

User Level Access Control

It is possible that Windows 95 has been installed and configured so that the Sharing tab on the properties dialog looks quite different from the picture above. This will occur only on Windows 95 computers that are members of a Novell or Windows NT network.

If your Sharing tab looks like this:

...then Windows 95 has been configured to use **User Level Access Control**. You will find that, instead of supplying a password for each share that you wish to control, you can grant access to specific users or **groups** of users on your network. This has a number of advantages, particularly if there are a large number of shared resources on the network. It means that any individual user does not have to remember a large number of different passwords for different resources, they have to remember only their password for logging on to the network as a whole.

However, because Windows 95 does not maintain a list of network users, it has to obtain the list from what is known as a security provider (which can be a Windows NT computer or domain, or a Novell Netware server), and hence has to be connected to one of these networks in order to do this.

If this is the case for your Windows 95 computer, try adding users to the permissions list for your share, by clicking

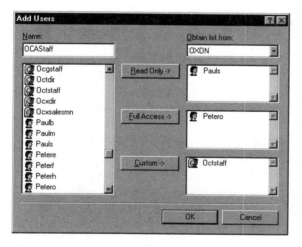

*It should be emphasised at this point, that any security you apply to your folders works **only for users connecting over the network**. It does not apply if someone sits down at your computer.*

– 177 –

Browsing the network

Now that you have set up a shared resource on your computer, it is time to see what other resources are accessible on the network (assuming, of course, that you are connected to one). We will assume that you are a member of a workgroup (for the sake of simplicity); if you are part of a client server network, very similar techniques will apply but the terminology and arrangement of computers will depend on the type of network.

🖰 *Open the 🖳 Network Neighborhood.*

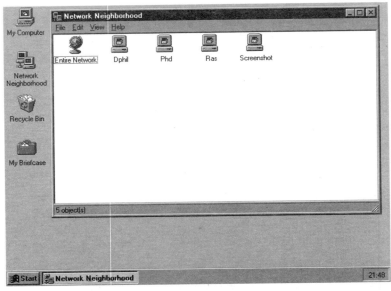

The window that you see here will display all the computers that your computer can see in your workgroup, plus an icon for the Entire Network (don't be surprised at the names given to computers, they can be called anything and often are). Note that when a machine is switched on, it will not appear in the 🖳 Network Neighborhood immediately. There may be other computers in your workgroup that yours has not noticed yet, these should appear after a short delay. Though a machine that does not have File and Print Sharing Services installed (see above) will never appear, not that this is much of a worry since there cannot be anything shared on such machines.

If you want to see which other workgroups are on the network, then you select the Entire Network. The idea behind this is to prevent you from being swamped by hundreds of computers that you have no great interest in, and to allow you to concentrate on machines in your 'neighborhood'. Once you have located the computer that has the resources you wish to use, you can open it to display all of its shared resources.

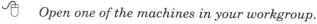 *Open one of the machines in your workgroup.*

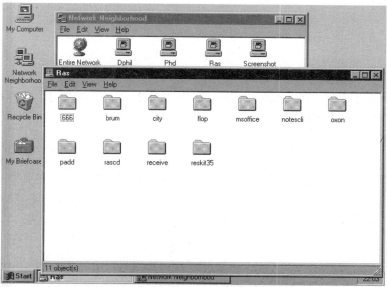

Assuming you have been granted access to the share, the shared folders that you can see now will behave largely as though they were on your own computer. If you have not been granted access, or if a password is required, you will be informed of the fact.

You will be able to edit documents and run programs, although you will find that programs run somewhat slower using files across the network. You can copy files from the share and, provided you have full access, copy files to the share. You can also copy folders from the share (and to it), but there is one important restriction: you cannot copy the shared folder itself. For example, assume there is a folder named SALESQ1 shared as SALES on a remote computer, and that the SALESQ1 folder has folders inside it named M1, M2 and M3. If you view the SALES share in the 🖳 Network Neighborhood, you will be able to drag and drop any of the folders M1, M2 or M3 on to your computer and make copies of them. You cannot, however, drag the icon for the SALES share (even though it looks like a folder) on to your computer and expect a copy to be made. Instead, Windows 95 offers to make a shortcut for you.

———— Network shortcuts ————

You can drag and drop a share from another computer to your desktop (using either mouse button) to create a shortcut to the network resource.

🖱 *From one of the machines you can see in the 🖳 Network Neighborhood, drag a folder for a share on to the desktop.*

You cannot move or copy the whole shared folder to your desktop; instead you must create a shortcut and are prompted to do so:

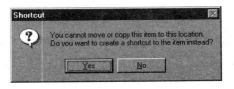

Click Yes

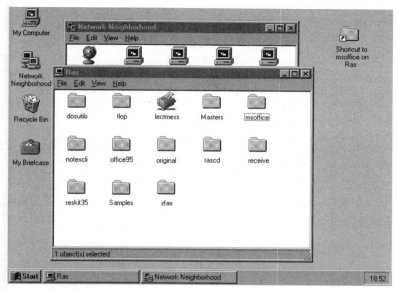

The shortcut allows you easy access to the files and folders stored in the shared folder. Note that, every time you log on to Windows 95 in future, the system will automatically try to connect to the network resource. If the shared folder cannot be reached, you will be given the option to discontinue further attempts to access the resource when logging on.

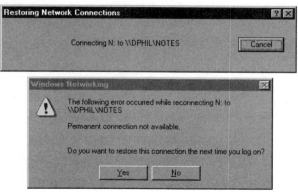

The advantage of shortcuts such as these is that you have a 'one-shot' way of getting to a shared folder on the network; you do not have to navigate through 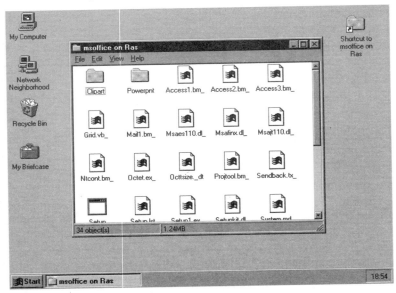 Network Neighborhood or the Explorer. To demonstrate this,

🖱️   *Close any open windows, then double-click the icon for the*
     shortcut you have just created on the desktop.

If you use many shared resources on your network and create shortcuts to each one, you may find your desktop getting rather cluttered. To solve this, you could create a folder on the desktop to contain all your network shortcuts. As with other folders, such folders cannot be created or moved into the Network Neighborhood or My Computer.

🖱️   *Close any open windows.*

Shortcuts to servers

As well as shortcuts to specific shared folders, you may find it
useful to have a shortcut to a server, allowing you to see any
shared resources on that computer.

👍 *In this context a server is any computer with a shared resource on it.*

Shortcuts to servers can be created in the 🖳 Network Neighborhood window. However, since each server already has an icon
in the window, server shortcuts are much more useful in another location, such as on the desktop.

🖰 *Open the* 🖳 *Network Neighborhood.*

Right-click one of the server icons.

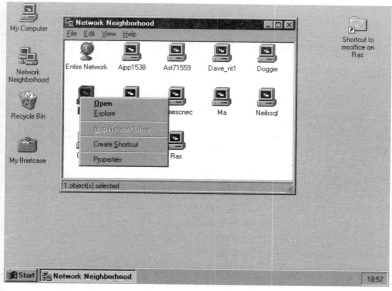

🖰 *Choose Create Shortcut.*

– 183 –

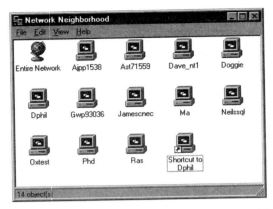

The shortcut has appeared in the 🖳 Network Neighborhood.

🖑 *Drag the shortcut icon to the desktop.*

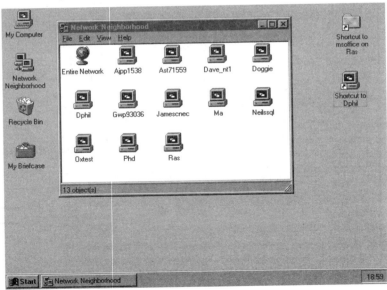

A quicker way to do this would be to drag the server icon from the Network Neighborhood on to the desktop.

🖱 *Drag a server to the desktop.*

You will be prompted to create a shortcut here.

🖱 *Click* [Yes]

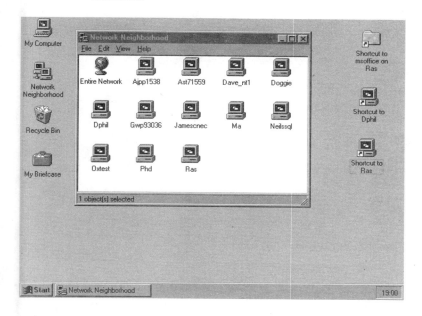

Mapping a drive to a shared network folder

If you are using an application that was not written for Windows 95, you may need to use drive letters to represent a shared network folder as such applications are not 'aware' of the Windows 95 🖧 Network Neighborhood. For example, the File Open dialog in Word 6 looks like this in Windows 95:

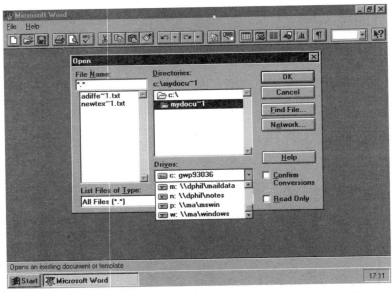

To choose a different shared folder, you must use the Drives: pull-down list and choose the drive letter which matches the share you are looking for.

Mapping a drive to a shared folder is a straightforward task in Windows 95.

🖱 *Right-click* 🖳 *My Computer or* 🖧 *Network Neighborhood.*

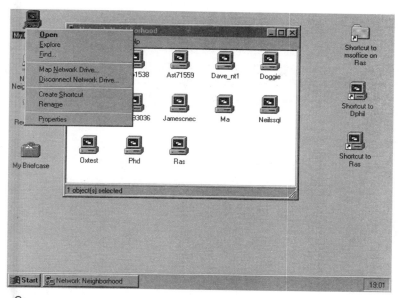

Choose Map <u>N</u>etwork Drive...

This is the standard Map Network Drive dialog. It contains pull down lists letting you specify which <u>D</u>rive letter you wish to use and which network share the drive refers to (the <u>P</u>ath). Note that there is no option to browse the network here; you need to know the appropriate path to the share.

☝ *You can use the pull down lists to see which drive letters are currently in use and which shares you have recently connected to and used.*

*Select a drive letter and use the Path: pull down list to
map this drive to one of the shared folders you used earlier.*

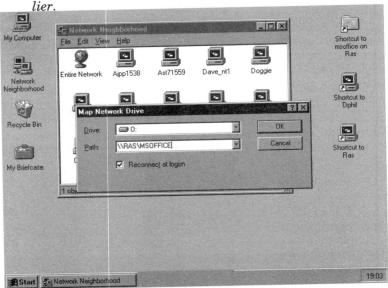

Notice ☑ **Reconnect at logon**. Leaving this checked means
that whenever you log on to Windows 95 it will automatically
try to map this drive letter to the same shared folder, saving
you the trouble of having to do it yourself.

Click OK

A window appears showing the contents of the share.

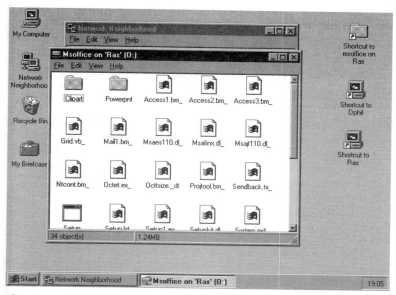

🖰   *Close the window.*

Nothing new appears on the desktop or in 🖳 Network Neighborhood as a result of mapping the drive, but there will be a new object in 🖳 My Computer.

🖰   *Open 🖳 My Computer.*

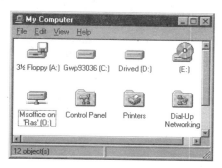

You should see an icon here for your connection to the network shared folder, with the share name, server name and drive letter all used for the icon title. The network connection icon you can see is different from the icon for a shortcut, even though in practice both objects will behave in a very similar way. Double-clicking the network connection would open a window displaying the contents of the share.

👍 *What if you have several Windows 95 network shortcuts and wish to use the same shared folders via a mapped drive (so that they could be used in Word 6 for example)? No problem. The context menu for a shortcut to a network shared folder contains a command to map a network drive to what the shortcut points to, or the shortcut's 'target'. If you were to choose this, the Map Network Drive dialog would appear with the Path already put in.*

Many peripheral devices which are attached to your computer, such as CD-Rom drives or printers, can be shared across the network in the same way as folders, and permanent connections to them can be created, as detailed above. Using shared network printers is discussed in the next chapter.

Tidying up the desktop

We will do this at this stage in the proceedings because you now have several icons on your desktop. You may feel happy with your desktop arrangement, and indeed the desktop is an ideal location for one or two shortcuts. However, just like your desk in the office, you can work more efficiently with a tidy desktop than one which is full of documents, folders and other objects. In general, you should strive to keep your Windows 95 desktop as organised as possible; folders help you to do this. As an exercise, you will create a Network Shortcuts folder on your C: drive to contain the shortcuts you have just created.

🖱 *Close any windows you have open, then start the Explorer. Click to select the C: drive in the left-hand pane of the Explorer window.*

The right-hand pane now shows the contents of your C: drive.
To create a new folder on the C: drive, you could right-click a
blank region of the right-hand pane and use the New submenu,
or you could use the File menu in the Explorer window. You
cannot choose New from the context menu of the C: drive icon.

> *Making sure that the C: drive is still selected in the Explorer window, click the File menu, and use the New submenu to create a new folder.*

This new folder on your C: drive will contain any shortcuts you
create to network resources.

> *Enter an appropriate name for the new folder, e.g. Network Shortcuts.*

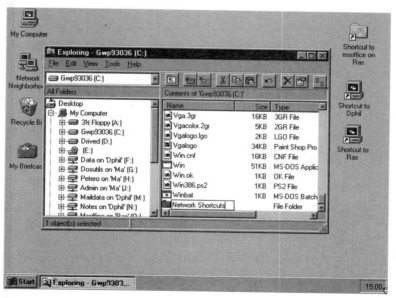

You can now drag the network shortcuts off your desktop into
this folder. It will be quicker to drag all the icons at once.

🖰 *Starting from an empty part of your desktop, drag the mouse to draw a rectangle which touches each network shortcut icon.*

This 'drag box' will select any icon it touches. You can see which icons are selected because they become highlighted.

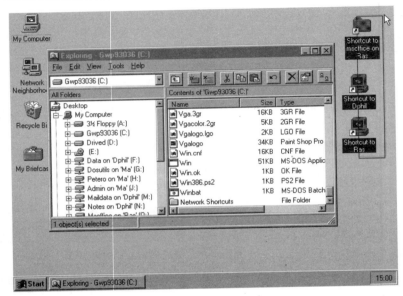

Dragging any one of the selected icons will drag the group.

🖰 *Drag the group of shortcuts into your Network Shortcuts folder.*

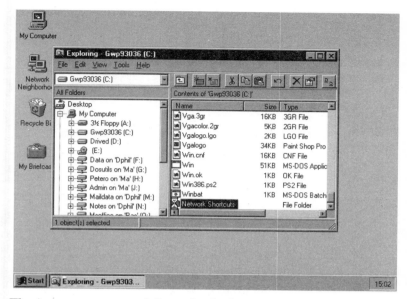

The icons are removed from the desktop.

🖱 *To get things really tidy, close any open windows and empty
the 🗑 Recycle Bin.*

Summary: The Network Neighborhood

- Using 🖳 Network Neighborhood enables the sharing of files and peripherals with other users.

- Right-clicking allows you to set share permissions
  on your own folders.

- Right-clicking network folders reveals their share
  permissions in the menu.

- You can create permanent connections to network
  resources using shortcuts on your desktop.

11

──USING PRINTERS──

This chapter covers:
- Using the Add Printer Wizard
- Creating shortcuts to printers
- Printing files using drag and drop
- Print management via printer windows

To print documents from your computer, you must first have access to a printer somewhere and then tell your computer to use the printer. You tell your computer which printer to use by '**adding**' or '**connecting**' a printer to it. You can connect either to a **local** printer (i.e. physically attached to a printer **port** at the back of your computer) or to a **remote** printer (a printer on a network).

We will assume for this chapter that you do have access to a printer. If the printer is connected directly to your computer, you will need to know the printer's make and model and which one of the ports at the back of your computer the printer is attached to. You can usually find this out by reading the label next to the port with the printer cable in it. If you use a printer over the network, you should not need to know what kind of printer it is, but you will need to know its location on the network.

Printers are added via the printer installation wizard which you access from the Start menu or from My Computer. This wizard asks you a series of questions about the location of your printer and what you would like it to be called. Using this information, the computer can install the printer for future use.

——————— Adding a printer ———————

This section assumes that you have a printer to install. If you have no printer, you can still go through most of the exercises, but you will have to cancel the last step, or wait for Windows 95 to display an error message of some sort when it fails to find the fictional printer.

✍️ *Click* 🟦Start *and move to the* Settings *submenu.*

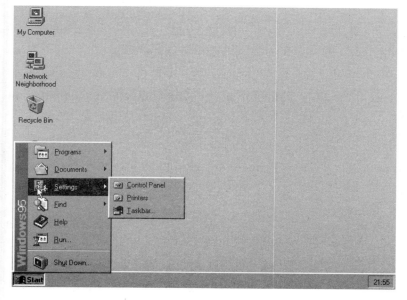

To add a new printer, or to view those that are already set up, you use a special object in Windows 95, the **Printers folder**. To open the Printers folder, choose the Printers option.

🖑 *Click Printers.*

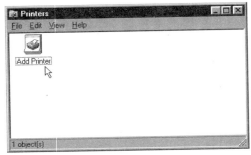

The Printers window is now displayed showing the contents of the Printers folder. This will contain icons for any printers you have installed on your computer. One reason why the Printers folder is regarded as 'special' in Windows 95 is that it always contains one object, the Add Printer icon, which you cannot delete (try it). To add a new printer you double-click this icon.

🖑 *Double-click the Add Printer icon.*

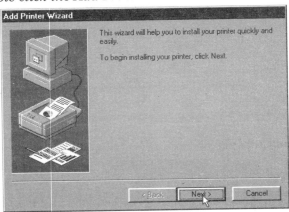

The Add Printer wizard begins. This will guide you step by step through the installation process for a local or remote printer. In the first step you are asked to begin installing your printer.

Click Next > *to continue installing your printer.*

The wizard then asks you how your printer is connected to your computer.

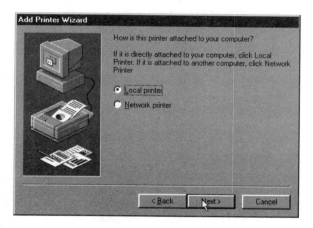

You have two choices: choose Local printer for a printer attached directly to the back of your computer, or Network printer for a printer attached to another computer on the network. Some of the differences between the two types of installation will be highlighted later.

Network printers

Choose Network printer and click Next >

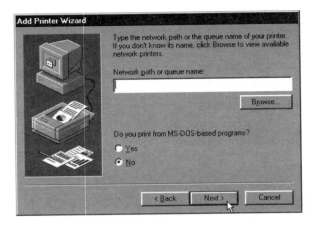

The wizard needs to know where the printer is on the network; you enter this information in the box labelled 'Network path or queue name'. If you are not sure of this information, in the format required, you can click Browse... and search the Network Neighborhood for the printer you want to connect to.

🖱️ *Click* Browse... *and locate the printer you want.*

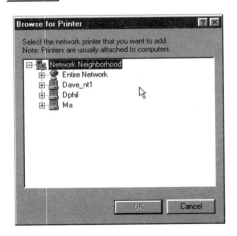

👍 *If you do not know where to look, it may be possible to ask a system administrator what you should enter here.*

The computer that the printer is connected to will be displayed under the 🖳 Network Neighborhood entry of the Browse for Printer window that you can now see.

🖱 *Click ⊞ next to the name of the computer to which the printer is attached to see a list of connected printers.*

👍 *Notice the similarity between this browse dialog and the left hand pane of the Explorer, an example of common user interface in action.*

The printers that are connected to this machine are shown. To add one, choose its name from the list.

🖱 *Choose a printer displayed in the list and click* <kbd>OK</kbd>

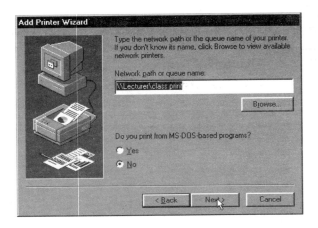

The correct path to the printer has been placed in the box.

> ⟨᷎ In the example above, the path was shown as a UNC (Universal Naming Convention) name. You may find the path displayed in a different manner on some types of network.

The next thing the Add Printer Wizard needs to know is if you wish to print from MS-DOS based programs. If you have any MS-DOS based programs that you print from you would choose ⊙ Yes now and follow instructions.

> ⟨᷎ If you choose to print from DOS based programs, you will be asked to 'capture' a printer port, typically LPT1 or LPT2. The reason for this is that DOS programs, by and large, have no conception of network printers. DOS programs will always print to local ports, but Windows 95 will redirect the output to the network printer.

🖱 *Leave the choice on* ⊙ *No and click* ▮ OK ▮

As this printer is a network-based printer, the machine that it is connected to tells your computer what sort of printer it is and the Wizard offers this as a suitable name. You can change this name if you wish.

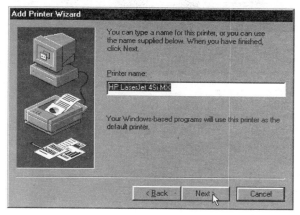

The name you choose will be used to refer to this printer within Windows 95. This name is usually some short description as to either what it can do or its location.

Choose a suitable name for the printer and type it in.

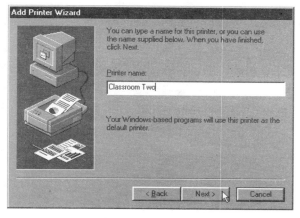

 *Click* Next >

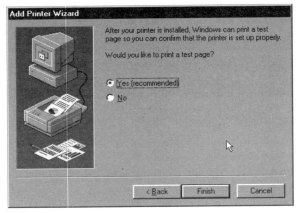

The final screen of the Add Printer wizard gives you the option
to print a test page to check that you are connected to the printer
correctly.

 *Leave ⊙ Yes (recommended) chosen and click* Finish *to
complete the installation of the printer.*

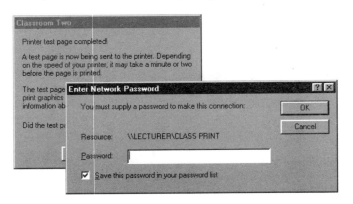

As the printer is connected across a network, to assist security, you may need to supply a password to gain access. This is to ensure that particular printers cannot be accessed if you do not know the password.

If you are asked for the password, type it in. If you do not know it you will have to click [Cancel] and possibly set the printer up later when you have access.

If you choose to print a test page, a confirmation of successful printing is displayed. If your test page is correctly printed then click [Yes] Choosing [No] will display the Printer Troubleshooter to help you diagnose possible printer problems.

A successful printer installation will result in a new printer icon displayed in the Printers window. This icon can now be treated just like any other application or file and a shortcut to it can be placed on the desktop.

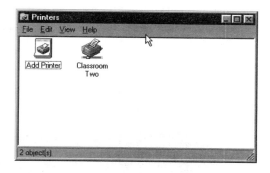

Local Printers

Adding a local printer differs only slightly from adding a network printer. In the Add Printer wizard, instead of choosing a path from where to choose the printer, you choose the printer manufacturer and model from a list.

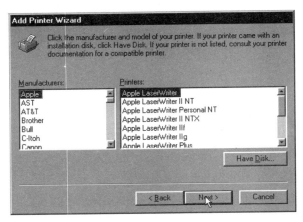

If your printer is not included on the list then you will need to have some software supplied by the manufacturer and will need to click ▭ Have Disk... ▭ to install the printer information for Windows 95.

Assuming the printer you want is on the list Windows 95 will install the software for it automatically.

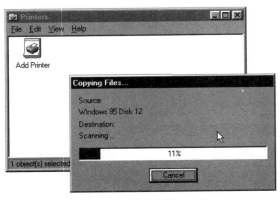

Once you have a printer attached directly to your computer you can share it as a network resource in the same way as you share a folder.

If you wish to share any locally connected printers then right-click the printer icon and choose Sharing...

Select ⦿ Shared As and supply a suitable Share Name and Comment.

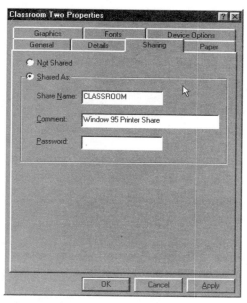

If you require some control over who uses this printer you should set up a password.

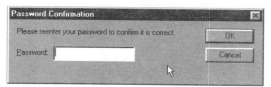

Your printer can now be used from other computers on the network.

Shortcuts to printers

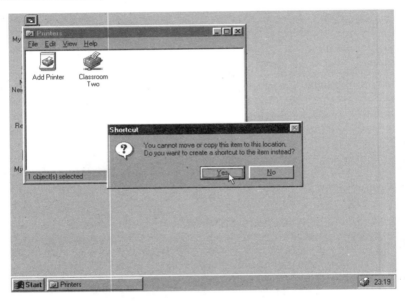

Drag the printer to the desktop using either the left or right mouse button.

If you use the left button you will be shown a dialog telling you that it cannot be moved and asking if you would like to create a shortcut instead.

Using the right mouse button will show you a menu allowing you to create a shortcut or to cancel the dragging of the printer.

> ᏇᏋ   *With items such as printers and disk drives which cannot be dragged out of their respective windows, either the left mouse button or the right mouse button will allow you to create a shortcut to another location.*

The printer is dropped where you release the mouse and called 'Shortcut to...' the name of the printer.

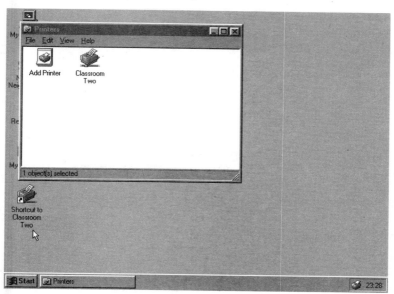

᠊ᠿ   *Rename the printer using a right-click and close the Printers window using* ✕

Classroom
Two

—— Printing files from the Explorer ——

You will often print a document by choosing the Print command in whichever application program you are working with. However, just as often you want to print a document that you are not working on. A very convenient feature when you wish to print a document from Windows 95 is the ability to drag a file (or more than one) on to the printer icon. For this reason it is a good idea to have a printer shortcut on your desktop.

Open an Explorer window and locate one of the text files you created earlier. They should be in your example folder, 'My Documents', on the C: drive.

Drag a file from the folder on to the printer icon on the desktop.

The application program that created this file is opened briefly and the file is printed; then the program is shut down again. If the program was already open, the document file is opened, printed, and closed, and the process is even quicker!

———— Managing print jobs ————

A document that has been sent to a printer will not always print immediately. There may be lots of other documents to be printed first, particularly on a network printer. In such cases the document is put into a **print queue**. A documents which is in a print queue is known as a **print job**. If you find that there is no need to print your document after all, or if someone else has a document which must be printed urgently, you may wish to delete or pause your print job. This can be done by opening a window for the printer the document was sent to.

The printer window

Printer windows display information about a printer. They can be used to check the printer status, for example, has the printer paused because of a problem, see which print jobs are in the print queue, and pause or delete your own print jobs.

☞ *Usually you can only manage your own print jobs. Certain people (print administrators) have the right to manage anyone's print jobs, and also to manage the printer.*

🖱 *Double-click the printer shortcut icon on the desktop.*

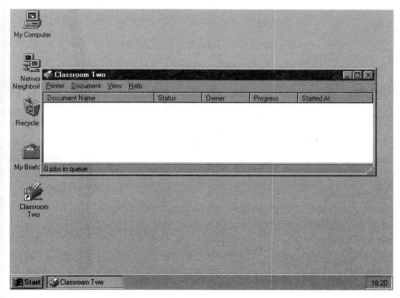

You may see your print job in the print queue, although by now the document may have been printed and the job taken off the queue.

🖑 *Drag a document on to the printer, as detailed above. Repeat this until you have several print jobs in the queue.*

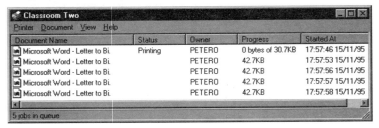

If you have the printer attached directly to your computer, you can use the Printer menu in this window to manage the printer.

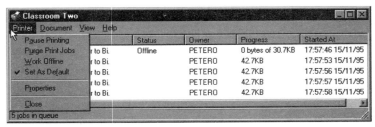

You can pause or cancel your own print jobs by selecting the job and then using the Document menu, or right-clicking the document icon for the print job.

🖑 *Right-click the icon for one of your print jobs.*

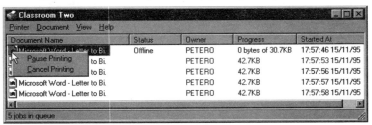

🖑 *Choose Cancel Printing from the context menu to delete the print job.*

Summary: Using Printers

- Printers can be set up locally and remotely using the Add Printer wizard.

- Local printers can be shared to allow others to access them, and security permissions can be enabled to allow only certain people, or those who know the password, to have access.

- You can print files by dragging the icon for the file on to the printer's icon.

12

USING THE HELP SYSTEM

This chapter covers:
- Getting into on-line Help
- Navigating around Help
- Annotating Help topics
- Searching for topics using the Index
- Using the Find facility
- The Help button

The first point to make about the Help system is its wide range of usefulness. Whether you are using Windows 95 for the first time or are an experienced user, the Windows 95 Help system is a powerful source of information. The Help system can be used to get information about particular applications you are running or about the Windows 95 environment in general. Each application should come with its own help file. Here you will be using the Help system to get information about using Windows 95.

 *Click* [Start] *then click* Help.

The Help Topics dialog appears, with three tabs, the first of which is Contents.

The Contents Tab

Five help icons are displayed; the icons in Help represent different parts of the Help system. The [?] icon represents a help **topic**, in this case 'Ten minutes to using Windows'. A topic contains the text of the help message, for example a description of what is meant by a certain phrase, or what an object is for, or instructions for carrying out specific tasks. Related help topics are grouped into categories, or **'books'**, shown by 📖. You can see that there is a book of topics on ' How to...' perform certain tasks. Books make it easier for you to find a topic.

You navigate through the Help system by selecting a book or topic, then clicking [Open] to open a book, [Close] to close a book or [Display] to open a topic, as appropriate. Alternatively you can double-click 📖 to open a book, double-click 📖 to close a book and double-click ? to open a topic.

🖱 *Click* 📖 *How to..., then click* [Open]

The 'How to...' book opens (notice the icon has changed to 📖). There are many books within this generic category.

🖱 *Double-click* 📖 *Run Programs.*

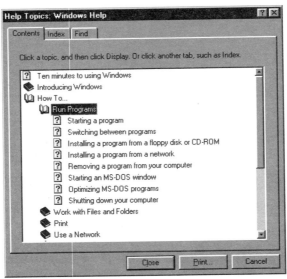

You are now presented with a list of topics related to running programs in Windows 95.

🖱 *Select a topic of interest, e.g.* ? *Starting a program, then click* [Display]

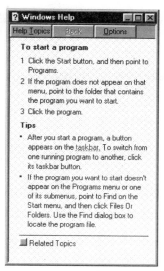

The 'Help Topics' dialog closes and a window appears with information on the topic you selected.

────────── Topic Windows ──────────

Each topic in the Windows 95 Help system is displayed in a sizeable window just like the one shown above. Just as with the Windows 3.x Help system, certain keywords appear in green text with a solid or dotted underline. Clicking these keywords will take you straight to the window for that topic or display a small **glossary** box to explain what the text means. Beneath the window's title bar are three buttons: Help Topics to return to the 'Help Topics' dialog; Back to take you back through the topics you have looked at; Options which, among other things, allows you print a topic, copy it to the clipboard or change the font for the text. Clicking a button at the bottom of the window will show you any topics related to the one you are looking at.

☝ ◾ *Related Topics only appears if there are any for the current topic.*

🖱 *Click ◾ Related Topics.*

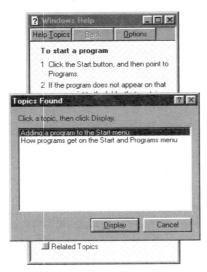

A list of similar topics is shown in a separate window. You could go to one of the related topics by selecting it then clicking Display or simply by double-clicking the topic.

🖱 *For now the related topics are not of interest, so click* ✕ *or* Cancel

——— Annotating help topics ———

You may add your own notes to the text of a help topic, by 'annotating' the topic. After adding an annotation, you will see a paper clip icon next to the topic heading.

🖰 *Click* [Options] *or right-click the topic window background.*

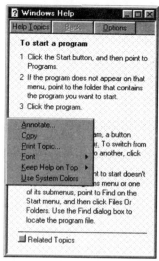

🖰 *Choose* Annotate... *Type in a helpful comment....*

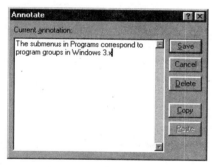

🖰 *and click* [Save]

Notice the paperclip icon near the top of the window. Clicking this displays the annotation for this topic. Annotations allow you to customise help topics. You can add your own explanations

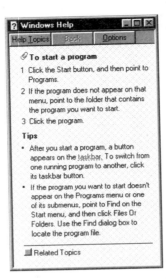

or cross-references if you feel they will make the text more relevant to the tasks you perform in Windows 95.

Now for the other tabs in the Help Topics dialog.

Click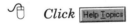

You should now be back at the original dialog, with the help topic window still open in the background.

The help index

The Contents tab you have just been using is useful if you are not sure exactly how to describe what you are looking for help on. If you want to go straight to the relevant topic window, and you know or can guess the topic title, it will be quicker in most cases to use the help Index tab.

🖱 *Click the Index tab.*

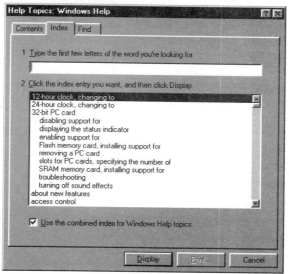

The index is an alphabetically sorted list of topics in the Help system. There are two stages. The first stage, which is optional, allows you to type in an entry to look for (or the first few letters). The Help system will then select the topic name that is the nearest match to what you have typed in. For example, typing **r** would select the topic 'read only files and folders', which is the first topic to begin with 'r'. Typing in **recy** would select Recycle Bin. You then scroll through the list (if necessary) in stage 2, select the topic of interest and click Display (or double click the topic).

For example, you might want to see what topics where available under the general topic heading 'running programs'.

🖱 *Type* **runn** *into the edit box.*

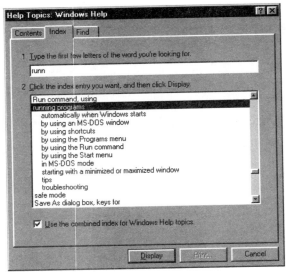

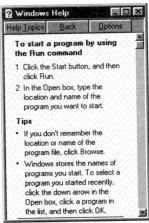

Select 'by using the Run command' and click [Display]

The dialog disappears and the help window shows the topic you
selected, in this case an alternative way of running a program
by using the Run command on the Start menu.

You will find that when you are using the Help system you will often look at one topic and then look at a related topic. In these cases you often want to go back and re-read the first topic in the light of something you found out in the second. Clicking  will make the window display the previous topic you looked at.

Click

Note that the annotation is still there, as shown by the paperclip icon.

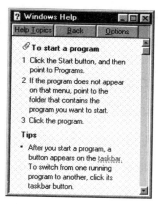

The 'Find' utility

The third tab in the Help system allows you to look up information according to key words and phrases.

Click Help Topics *to return to the Help Topics dialog, then click the Find tab.*

The first time you click the Find tab you will need to wait a short while for a list of topics and keywords to be compiled by the system from the various Windows 95 help files.

You can either let Windows 95 build the list for you (the default, recommended option), or choose which help files to include in a custom list.

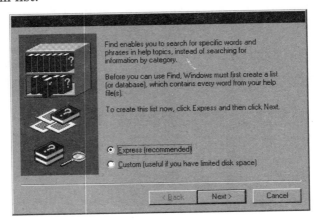

First, have a look which help files are available.

To see which help files can be included, click ○ Custom, then click Next >

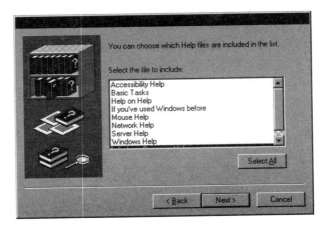

You may not be sure which of these files contains the information you are seeking, so it may be better to let Windows 95 build the list for you.

 *Click* < Back

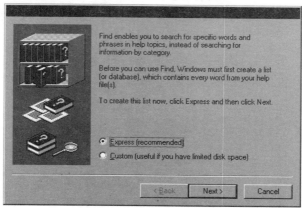

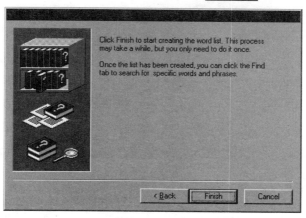

As indicated by the dialog, the list of topics will take a short while to build, but this only has to be done once.

 *Click* Finish

The index will now be built for you.

Eventually, the Help Topics dialog is redrawn, with the Find tab active.

The idea here is that you can 'home in on' a topic of interest by typing in key words and phrases in the edit box. This is stage 1. At the moment, nothing has been entered. The list of matching words in stage 2, rather than displaying nothing, shows the complete list. Likewise, the list of topics in stage 3 displays the complete set of topics. You can see from the bottom left of the dialog how many matching topics have been found (361 in the screenshot above).

As an example, assume you want to find help about folders in Windows 95, and in particular how to create them.

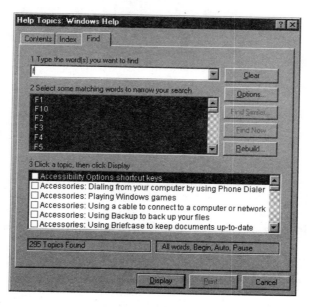 Type **f** into the edit box.

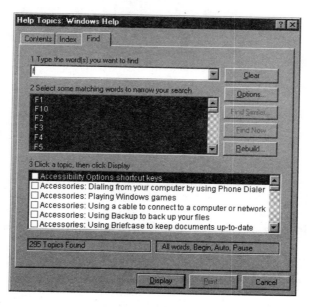

The list of matching words in stage 2 changes accordingly, to any keywords beginning with 'f'. Notice that this hasn't narrowed down the range of topics a great deal!

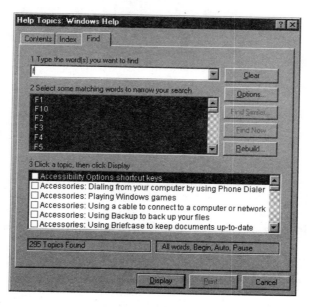 Now complete the word **folder**.

As you type, the lists update almost immediately.

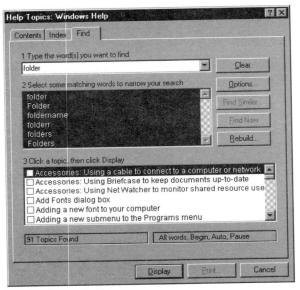

The search is starting to converge! There are only a few matching keywords now, but there are still 91 topics found. This is because the topics listed may not relate directly to creating and using folders, but the text in the topic contains the word 'folder'.

🖰 *Click to select the first matching word in the list, 'folder'. (The case is significant here.)*

Seventy-five matching topics are displayed, some of which don't appear to have much relevance to folders. What would happen if we tried 'Folder'? Selecting 'folder' will show you a list of topics which contain the word 'folder' somewhere in the text, whereas selecting 'Folder' displays topics considered to relate directly to the concept of a folder.

🖰 *Now select 'Folder'.*

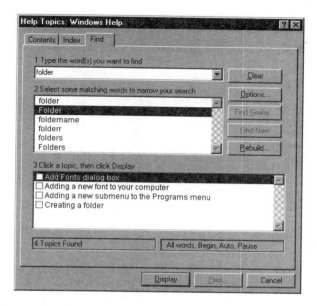

This time only four topics are displayed. Remember that you are interested in how to create a folder.

Select 'Creating a folder' (you do not have to check ▢). Now click Display

The appropriate help topic is shown.

🖰 *Click* ▄ *Related Topics.*

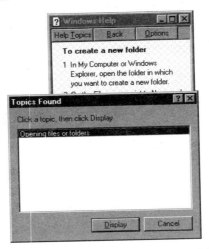

There is one related topic: Opening files or folders.

🖰 *Click* ❌ *or* [Cancel] *to close the Topics Found dialog.*

Perhaps you wanted more choice of related topics. This can be done from the Help Topics window.

🖰 *Click* [Help Topics]

The Help Topics dialog reappears.

🖰 *Check* ☑ *Creating a folder.*

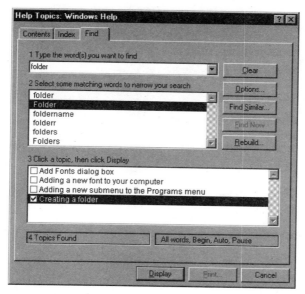

Notice that  is now available.

🖱 *Click* Find Similar...

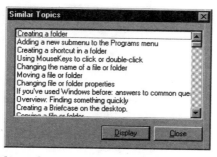

An extensive list of topics similar to the topic you checked appears.

🖱 *Select 'Changing the name ...' then click* Display

– 229 –

Click  *to go back to the Similar Topics window and close the window.*

Find options

You may have been wondering what determines which topics and key words are listed when using the Find tab.

Click

This dialog allows you to control which key words appear:

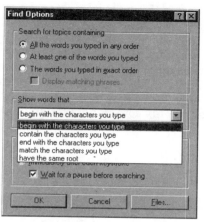

If you know which help files you are interested in you can exclude the others by clicking [Files...]

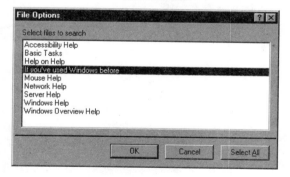

Using the techniques above to narrow the scope of the search can considerably speed up finding the desired information in the Help system.

Keep clicking ✖ until you have closed the Help system.

'What's This?' and the help button

You should be aware by now that right-clicking is an important technique when using Windows 95. This is no difference in the Help system. Right-clicking will usually bring up a context menu of commands associated with whatever you are pointing at. On other occasions the only command available is 'What's This?'.

🖱 *Restart Help from the Start menu and click the Contents tab. Right-click somewhere in the list, e.g. a book icon* 📚

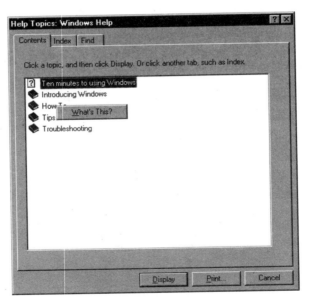

🖱 *Click 'What's This?' in the context menu.*

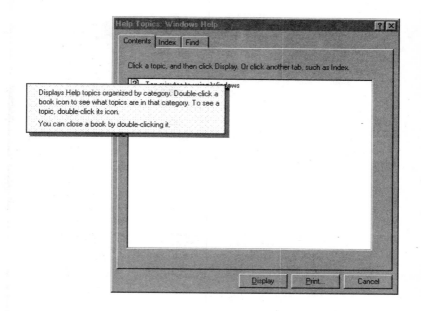

A text box appears explaining what the icons in the list are for.

☞ *Note that not everything you can click will have an associated text box.*

An alternative way of getting these help text boxes is to use the help button **?**.

🖱 *Click* **?**

Notice the new mouse pointer.

🖱 *Click something else, e.g.* **Display**

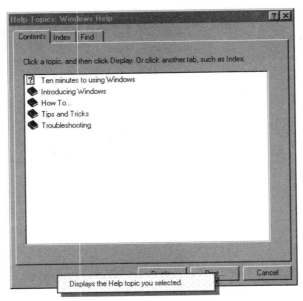

Again a text box appears containing help on whatever you clicked.

🖱 *Click* ❌ *or* Cancel *to exit the Help system.*

Getting help in dialogs

'What's This?' and will often work in just the same way when you are looking at a dialog, for example the Taskbar Properties dialog.

🖱 *Right-click the Taskbar and choose Properties...*

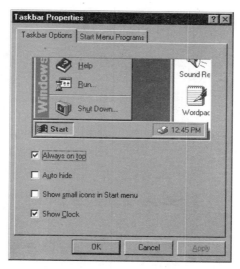

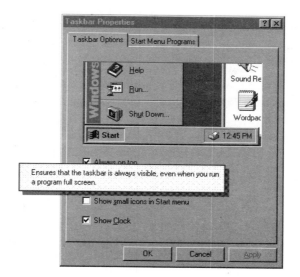

Right-click '☑Always on top' and choose 'What's This?' from the context menu:

Now click 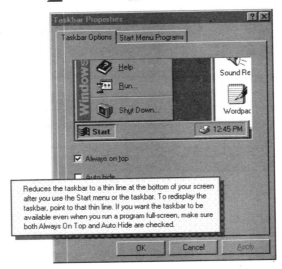 *and click ☐ Auto hide:*

Note that only works within the dialog. You cannot click and then click something on the desktop, such as 🖥 My Computer.

Summary: Using the Help System

- The Help system can be started from the Taskbar.

- Help topics can be accessed from a tabbed dialog box via different routes.

- There is a structure of 'books' and topics, which can be activated by double-clicking the appropriate icon.

- You can search for topics in the help index, an alphabetical list of all the topics in the system.

- There is a powerful 'find' utility to search for key words or phrases, and look up related topics.

- Information on many parts of the Windows 95 interface can be obtained by clicking the help button or selecting 'What's this?' from the context menu.

13

—— FINDING FILES ——

This chapter covers:
- How to locate a file
- Using different search methods

The 'Find' utility in Windows 95 can be used for two purposes: finding a computer on the network; and finding a file or a folder. It is the second of these that you will concentrate on in this chapter.

Earlier in the book we presented some guidelines for how to structure your file storage on your computer. Without a logical structure you may end up with no idea where you saved that important report you were working on, or even what it was called. This is what the Find utility was designed for. You can search for files by name or date of creation/modification, or look for files containing a certain piece of text.

It is possible to search for a file anywhere that can be accessed from ▣ My Computer. You can look in everything in ▣ My Computer, although if you have lots of network connections searching for a file on lots of computers around the network

would be very slow. It is far more efficient to search in a particular location, assuming you have a vague idea of where to
begin the search, such as your computer's C: drive. You can
select the location to search in before activating the Find dialog. To do this you would choose Find from the context menu of
the icon for the appropriate object, e.g. your C: drive, or a network drive. An alternative would be to choose Find from the
Tools menu in the Windows 95 Explorer, with the location selected. For this chapter, you will use the most general method:
the Start menu.

—————— Finding a file by title ——————

🖰   *Click* ▓▓**Start** *and choose* Files and Folders... *from the* Find
     menu.

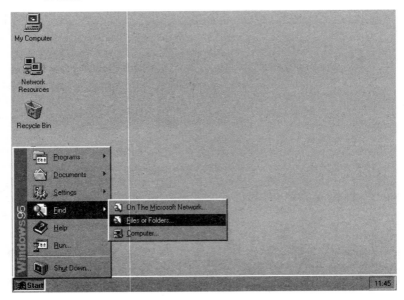

You are presented with a dialog box asking for the name of the file that you wish to search for and where to look for your file.

    Note that it does not matter what case you use to type in the filename as the search is not case sensitive for filenames.

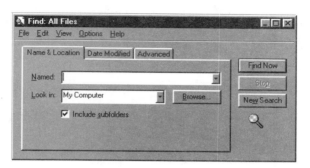

You will use this dialog box to search for the CIRCLES file, used earlier. The file is likely to be on the C: drive. Make sure the ☑ **Include subfolders** option is set, as this will search all subdirectories for the file as well.

    You can choose to search in a particular folder on a drive. Clicking will open an Explorer-style dialog for you to select the folder on a local or network drive.

    Type circles *into the 'Named:' box and choose to Look in the C: drive.*

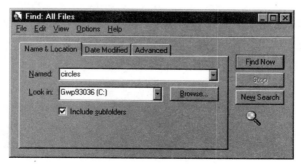

🖱 Click on ▌Find Now▐

While Windows 95 is searching for the file the magnifying glass which appears on the right of the dialog box will rotate around a piece of paper, indicating that the search is in progress. As files are found that match the search criteria their name and location appear in the bottom portion of the dialog. If one of these is the file you are searching for you can click on ▌ Stop ▐ at that point.

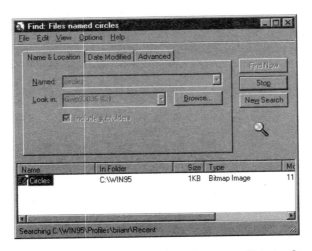

The information about the files found cannot fit into the default-sized Find Files dialog. If necessary, click on the right scroll bar to see the date that the file was last modified. To open any of the files that the search has located, double-click the icon at the far left of the filename. You can also use context menus to work with the files found in the dialog:

🖰 *Click on* New Search *to clear the window, then click on* OK *to confirm that you want to clear the current search.*

———— Other search methods ————

Other methods within the Find dialog can be used to search for particular files. By clicking the 'Date Modified' tab, a list of options is given allowing you to search for files that have been modified on a particular day, between a set of dates, or within a timescale.

🖰 *Click the Date Modified tab.*

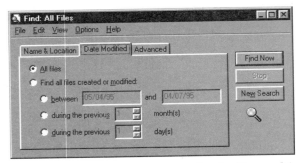

The 'Advanced' tab offers yet more methods of searching.

🖰 *Click the Advanced tab.*

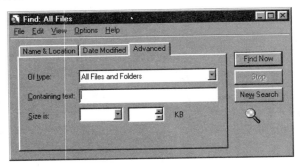

Using this option allows files to be searched for by type, or size range, for example 'at most 500K'. A nice feature is that you can look for any files that contain a particular piece of text. If you wish to take advantage of this feature, you will be pleased to know that searching for text in a file is not case sensitive by default. This means that the computer will ignore the case of your search request when trying to match it with text in a file. If it is important that the search is case sensitive then this can be changed using the Case Sensitive command on the Options menu. Searching for a file based on a piece of text it contains will be slower than searching for a file by its name.

Note that the search criteria you enter into each tab in the Find dialog will be combined in the final search. For example, you could choose to search for a file in the My Documents folder which was created during the last week and contains the text 'Oxford Computer Training'.

Summary: Finding Files

- 'Find' can be used to search for the location of files or folders, or to find a computer on the network.

- Within the Find dialog you can use the context menu to manipulate the files which are found.

- Files or folders can be searched for by name, by filesize, by filetype, modification date, or by words contained in the file.

14

— THE BRIEFCASE —

This chapter covers:

- What 💼 My Briefcase is
- Why you would use 💼 My Briefcase
- How to use this feature

— What the Briefcase provides —

It is quite commonplace now for people to do work on more than one computer. For example, you may have a computer on your desk in the office and a portable computer to take with you when you are out of the office. You may also have your own computer at home which you sometimes use to work with documents from the office. It can be quite tiresome to ensure that each computer you use has the latest copy of the document you are working on.

For example, you may start writing a report on your desktop computer in the office, add to a copy of it on your portable during the train journey home and finish it using a third copy on your computer at home that evening. If you take several days to write the report it is all too easy to lose track of where the latest copy is. This is where 💼 My Briefcase comes in.

The concept is quite elegant. You put a **copy** of a document into 💼 My Briefcase on your desktop computer. You then **move** 💼 My Briefcase on to your portable computer or on to a floppy disk to be transferred to another computer later. You now have a copy of your document in 💼 My Briefcase, and the original (at work). You can make changes at home to the copy in My Briefcase. Later you transfer the Briefcase back to your office computer and Windows 95 synchronises the original with the copy in the Briefcase.

💼 My Briefcase will therefore synchronise the contents of two sets of files, the originals and the copies held in 💼 My Briefcase. It is important to understand that the contents of 💼 My Briefcase are only copies of the original files. Windows 95 attaches hidden information to these files which allows it to find the originals later and overwrite whichever version you choose.

As with so many of the new tools available with Windows 95, the Briefcase is designed to be as user friendly as possible. Data can be transferred either by floppy disk (as in the following example) or by direct cable connection (as described in the Help section "About Briefcase" / "Related Topics").

Moving data to the Briefcase

Open the Explorer and restore it (i.e. so that you can see the Briefcase icon, as on the next page).

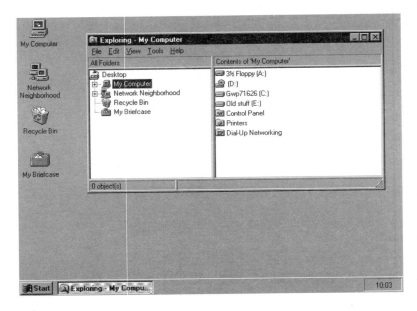

The files you want to transfer can simply be dragged on to 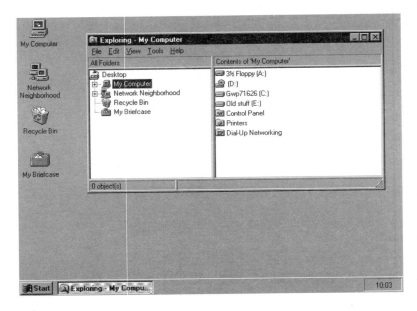 My Briefcase on the desktop. Alternatively, by right-clicking the file you want to move you can select 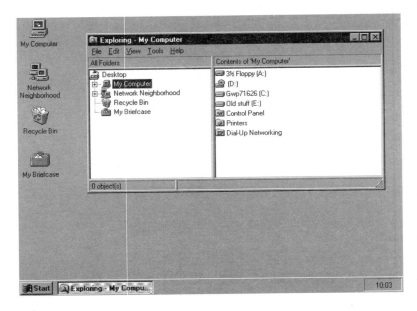 My Briefcase from the destinations in the Se<u>n</u>d To list on the context menu.

By clicking the ⊞ symbol beside 🖳 My Computer and the C: drive you will be able to see the Windows 95 installation folder.

🖰 *Click Win95 to display the directory contents in the right-hand pane of the window.*

🖰 *Drag the* CLOUDS *file out of Explorer and drop it on to* 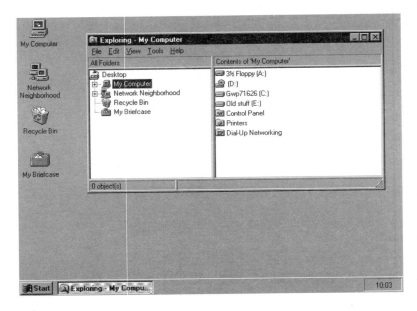 *My Briefcase on the desktop.*

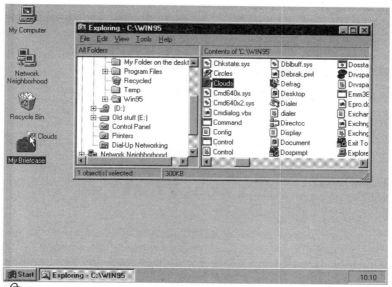

Do the same thing with the TIPS file (in the same directory).

Having placed your files in 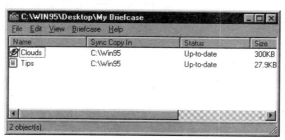 My Briefcase, you can open it with a double-click and confirm the contents.

Double-click My Briefcase.

You can see the files you have just sent to the Briefcase.

From the View menu, choose to see the Details of each file.

Notice that the **Status** of the files is 'Up-to-date', i.e. there are no differences between the copies in My Briefcase and the original files.

Moving My Briefcase
to a floppy disk

If you wanted to take home a copy of these documents from the office, you could put the copies on to a floppy disk. To make sure that only files which you have changed that day in the office will be transferred on to your home computer, you should move My Briefcase to the floppy and then put it on to your home computer. You can move My Briefcase from the desktop to a floppy disk by dragging the icon or choosing 3 ½ Floppy (A) from Send to on the My Briefcase context menu. My Briefcase must be closed before it can be moved

Close My Briefcase and Explorer.

Insert a floppy disk in Drive A:.

Right-click My Briefcase to bring up the context menu.

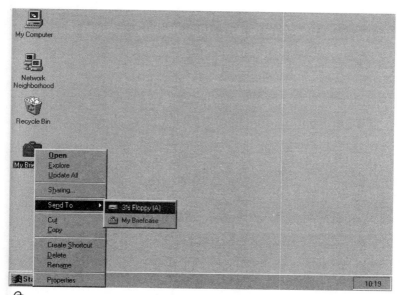

🖰 *From the menu choose Send To and then click the 3 ½ Floppy (A) option.*

You will see an animated dialog as 💼 My Briefcase and its contents are moved to the floppy disk.

Note that, unlike most other files, the default send to mode for the Briefcase is move, even though it is being transferred between drives. It is important to remember that you should never copy a Briefcase, otherwise you will have two copies of files independently synchronising with the original but not synchronising with themselves.

With the whole of 💼 My Briefcase on the floppy disk you could now open some of the original documents and make changes to them. This will allow you to watch the synchronisation process later.

🖱 *Open Explorer and double-click* CLOUDS *in the Win95 folder. The file will be opened automatically for you.*

Make some obvious changes to the picture.

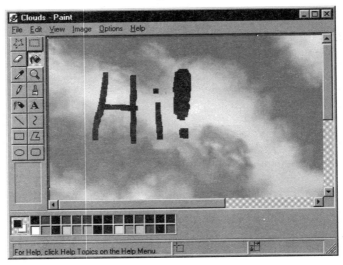

🖱 *Close Paint and click* Yes *to save the changes to the file.*

The other file, TIPS, is a text document.

🖱 *Open* TIPS *and make some changes that you will recognise later.*

Close the document.

👍 *Remember to save the changes when you close.*

——————— Synchronising files ———————

From Explorer you can access the contents of the floppy disk.

🖱 *Go to Explorer and click on the 3½ Floppy (A:) object in the left pane of the window.*

Simply dragging the Briefcase object from the A: drive to the desktop will move it back there. Note that you cannot specify the desktop as a location in Se*n*d to on the context menu for a Briefcase on a floppy disk.

🖱 *Drag the Briefcase object from the right pane of the Explorer window to the desktop.*

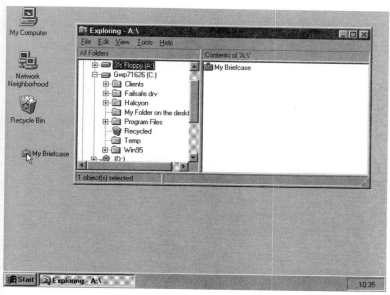

Note again that during a drag and drop operation the Briefcase is moved by default and not copied.

🖰 *Minimise the Explorer.*

Double-click 📁 *My Briefcase. Choose Details from the View menu in the window.*

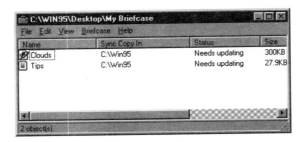

You will see in the window that the status of the files has changed to 'Needs updating'. Windows 95 has detected that these files are now different from the originals.

If you decide to update the files, Windows 95 will suggest that you overwrite the older versions with the more recent.

🖰 *From the Briefcase menu choose Update All...*

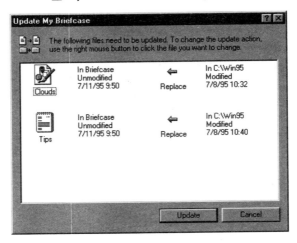

This dialog contains a graphical representation of which of the pair of files (the original and the copy) will be updated. The arrow indicates which file will overwrite the other.

As the dialog tells you, you can right-click and use the context menu to change the direction of the update, or to skip the update for certain pairs of files if you are not confident of which you wish to keep.

👆 *You can synchronise selected pairs of files rather than all files by clicking the document icon at the left of the window and choosing Update Selection from the Briefcase menu.*

🖱 *Click*

The files will now have been synchronised to the most recent version.

🖱 *Check in the My Briefcase window that the status now reads Up-to-date.*

Open one of the files in 💼 *My Briefcase to satisfy yourself that your modified version has been copied to the Briefcase.*

Deleting one of the files

If you put a copy of a file in the Briefcase and subsequently delete the original file or delete the file in your briefcase, various results may ensue.

Case 1

You do not change either file. If you delete the copy in the Briefcase and then choose Update All, the Briefcase will suggest that you delete the original file as well. If this is not what you wish to do, you will need to right-click and choose create. If you delete the original, then the Update All option will suggest you delete the copy in your Briefcase.

Case 2

You change the original file. If you delete the copy in your Brief-case, you will find the Update <u>A</u>ll option produces the message 'The Briefcase cannot find any files that need updating. All of your files are up to date.' If you delete the original, Update <u>A</u>ll will suggest that you delete the copy in your Briefcase as well. You can right-click and choose create if you wish.

Case 3

You change the file in the Briefcase. If you delete the original, after Update <u>A</u>ll, you get the message 'The files in the Briefcase are orphans. They will not be updated.' If you delete the Brief-case copy, then Update <u>A</u>ll will suggest that you delete the origi-nal file as well. Again, this can be changed by right-clicking and choosing create.

Other options

Merge

When updating files in the Briefcase, the context menu in the update dialog offers various options which we have already de-scribed. There is one further option which you may see for some types of document, **merge**.

This option will be presented only for documents of an applica-tion that supports a feature allowing its documents to be merged together, e.g. Access 7. The Briefcase itself cannot merge docu-ments, it must ask the application that created the documents to do it. Do not confuse this feature with mail merge in word processor applications. Merge in this context involves creating a combined document containing the newer parts of the two con-tributory documents. What constitutes a *part* depends on the type of document – it could be a cell in a spreadsheet, a para-graph in a word processor or a record in a database. At the time of writing, Access 7 is the only application that supports such a feature.

Multiple Briefcases and Renaming

Why would you want to have more than one Briefcase? Well, you may have more than just two computers for which you wish to synchronise files, for example, the one on your desk in the office, one at home, and possibly a computer you frequently use when visiting a client. It would be beneficial to have a different briefcase for different situations: one for synchronising a set of files between home and the office, another to synchronise a different set of files between your office and the client's.

A new Briefcase can be created in a chosen location on your computer, such as the My Documents folder, in a similar way to a document or shortcut, i.e. from the context menu or File menu in the appropriate window. The default name is ![briefcase icon] New Briefcase.

You can create many different Briefcases in Windows 95, but to avoid confusion you should make sure that each has a different name. Note that, as with all objects, if you create two Briefcases in the same folder, they cannot have the same name. You rename a Briefcase in just the same way as you would rename other objects in Windows 95, e.g. by choosing Rename from the context menu for the Briefcase or clicking the name area.

That having been said, care should be exercised when working with multiple Briefcases as it is easy to set up situations in which you are trying to synchronise too many copies of documents. Microsoft recommend that you stick with one Briefcase wherever possible.

Multiple users

A Briefcase can be part of a user's profile. As we have mentioned earlier, if Windows 95 is configured appropriately, different users can have their own settings on a single machine. Therefore different users can have their own Briefcases.

Summary: The Briefcase

- The Briefcase is a powerful means of synchronising files which are used in more than one place, or by a number of different people.

- The whole of the Briefcase (*not* just its contents) is removed from the desktop to the floppy disk by dragging and dropping or via Se<u>n</u>d to on the context menu.

- You put My Briefcase back on to the desktop of your computer using drag and drop.

- Windows 95 will indicate if file synchronisation is necessary; you choose which version of a file you wish to keep.

- You can use many different Briefcases if you wish, but you would be wise to give each a different name.

15

CUSTOMISING THE START MENU

<hr>

This chapter covers:
- Adding new items via Taskbar Properties
- Adding new menu items using drag & drop
- Adding new items via Explorer / My Computer
- Deleting items from the Start menu

<hr>

Start menu items

Most items on the Start menu are put there automatically by Windows 95. **Shut Down, Run, Help, Find, Settings** and **Documents** are all fixed items provided by the standard installation. However, some customisation is possible.

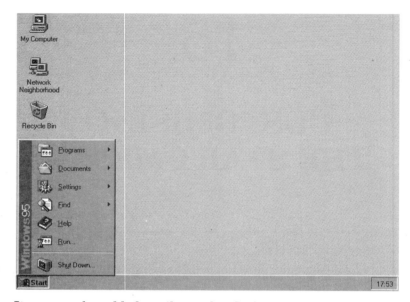

Items can be added easily to the **Start** menu, the **Programs** submenu and further submenus in Programs such as **Accessories**. This can be done in a number of ways: via a properties dialog box, or using drag and drop into a window or on to.

Any items which you put into the Start menu structure will be stored in a special **folder**. There is a hierarchical structure of folders within folders, starting from the Start Menu folder, that reflects the hierarchical structure of the Start menu itself. For example, there is a **Start Menu** folder, which will contain a **Programs** folder for the Programs submenu, which in turn contains a folder for each submenu such as Accessories.

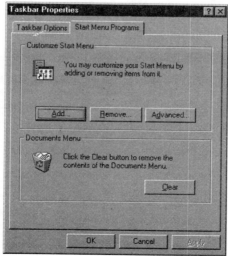

It is possible for a systems administrator to configure Windows 95 so that some (or indeed all!) Start menu options are unavailable. If your Start menu is different from the ones portrayed in this book, you may have to contact your systems administrator to find out why. It is also worth noting that some applications, e.g. Office 95, add their own items to the Start menu during installation.

Adding new items via Taskbar Properties

The Taskbar Properties dialog can be accessed from the Start menu or from the Taskbar's context menu. The dialog has two tabs: Taskbar Options and Start menu Programs.

Click **Start** and select _Settings_ followed by _Taskbar...._

👆 *The Taskbar Options tab defines Taskbar operation and appearance, and was discussed in an earlier chapter,.*

🖰 *Select the Start Menu Programs tab.*

👆 *To switch between tabs on a dialog -use* `Ctrl`-`Tab` *to step through to the desired page.*

Note that there are two sections to this dialog, the lower section is for clearing the contents of the Documents submenu. The upper section allows the user to Add / Remove menu items via dialogs or perform Advanced actions via the Explorer.

🖰 *Click*

This dialog takes the form of a Windows 95 wizard, leading the user step by step through the process of adding a menu item. Note that the item is described as a shortcut. Menus and submenus are folders, but generally only shortcuts should be stored within them.

The command line for the program you wish to run should be supplied. You are going to add a menu item for Notepad to the Programs submenu.

🖰 *For the Command line, type* `notepad`.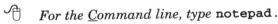

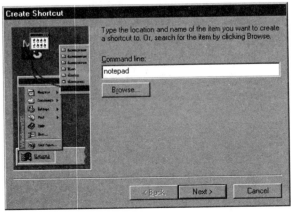

If the Command line is not known you may find it helpful to use to explore.

> ☞ *Only executable file names or documents are allowed. It is not possible to access DOS commands such as 'dir' directly from a short-cut, although DOS applications and utilities can be added.*

The wizard finds and inserts the full path for the Notepad executable file, i.e. the program, then moves to the next stage of creating a menu item - placing the item in the correct menu. The dialog for this displays the options available in a hierarchical structure, just like the Explorer, and allows the user to select the desired menu by clicking the icons. Note that you may only customise the Programs submenu, and any submenus it contains, or the Start menu itself. All the menus shown here are folders. If a suitable submenu is not present, it is possible to add one by adding a new folder. For the time being you will add Notepad to the Programs submenu.

🖰 *Select Programs and click* Next > .

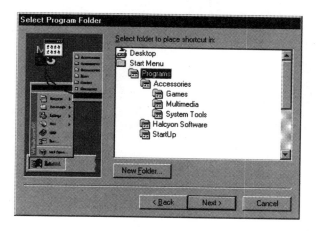

The penultimate step is to give the menu item a name. This should be as brief and logical as possible. It is possible to add long, descriptive names but it should be borne in mind that this will not necessarily enhance the menu design, for example:

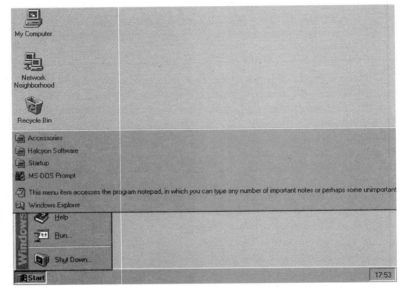

🖑 *Call the item* **Notepad**, *and click* Finish

Now to try the new menu.

🖑 *Click* 🏁 Start *and select* Programs.

Your list of menu items should include Notepad. If you select it, a window will open with Notepad ready to use.

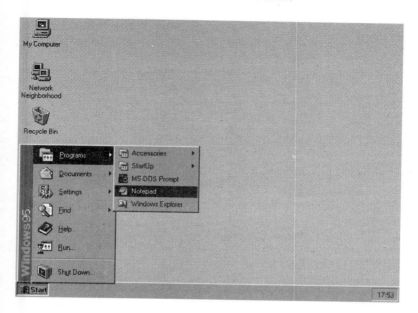

── Adding items using drag & drop ──

An item may be added to the Start menu itself by dragging the item and dropping it on ⊞Start. As an example, you shall add the Explorer to the top of the Start menu. First you must locate the application file for the Explorer.

🖑 *Click* ⊞Start *and select* Find, *then* Files or Folders. *Type* **Explorer,** *check that 'Look in:' is set to C: and that Include subfolders is checked.*

Click Find Now

Find will locate all instances of Explorer, including shortcuts. You must pick the application item (look in the Type column in the Find dialog). To add this item to the Start menu you need to drag it, using either mouse button, and drop it on ⊞Start.

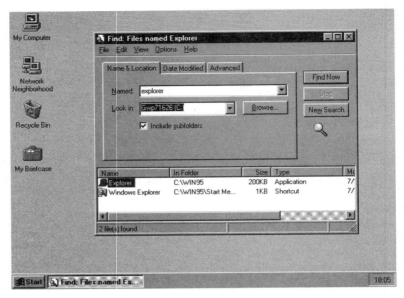

🖰 *Select the application Explorer (*EXPLORER.EXE*) and, holding down either mouse button, drag it to* 🏁Start*. Release the mouse.*

👍 *This can be achieved even if the taskbar is hidden by Autohide. Simply drag the file to the edge of the screen and pause while the taskbar reappears.*

Note that by doing this you are not moving the Explorer to the Start menu; you are creating a shortcut to it in the Start menu folder.

🖰 *Click* 🏁Start *to confirm that Explorer is on the Start menu.*

Adding items to the Start menu window

There is yet another way of adding items to the Start menu. Anything which you put on the Start menu, or the Programs submenu, will go in the corresponding folder. You can look at the contents of any of these folders by opening a window on them. Items can then be added by manually creating or dragging folders and shortcuts into the folder window.

The easiest way to open a window for the Start menu folder is via the context menu for the Start button.

 Right-click **Start** and choose **Open**.

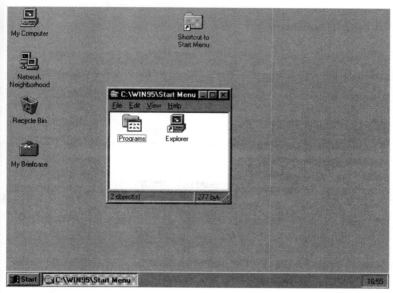

Items can be added to this window in the usual ways. You can choose one of the objects in the New submenu of the File menu, or on the context menu if you right-click the window background.

Items can be moved or copied from either the Explorer or anywhere in 🖥 My Computer, using the standard drag & drop methods.

🖰 *Drag the Explorer icon out of the Start menu window to the desktop, and open the Start menu itself to see the effect.*

The Explorer should no longer be there.

🖰 *Drag the Explorer shortcut back into the Start menu window to reinstate it.*

You could open the Programs folder to add items there, or create new submenus by creating folders in a suitable part of the hierarchy.

🖰 *If you wish, add other items to the Start menu structure by dragging them to the appropriate folder.*

When you have done adding items, close the Start Menu window.

Ad̲vanced... in the Taskbar Properties dialog (Start Menu Items tab) will open an Explorer window with the Start Menu folder at the top of the hierarchy. Shortcuts on the Start menu can be manipulated from here too.

Deleting Items from the Start menu

Items can be deleted from the Start menu in different ways: using the Taskbar Properties dialog box, or from the window for the Start menu folder, or using the Explorer to access the Start menu folder. To try this, you will delete the menu item Notepad you added earlier in the chapter from the Taskbar property sheet.

Right click the taskbar and select Properties. This accesses the Taskbar Properties dialog box seen earlier. Select the Start Menu Programs tab.

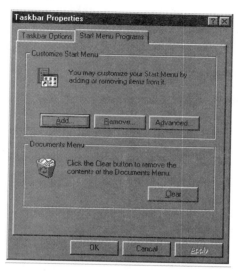

Click on

This screen shows you the items contained in the Start menu. Any item shown here can be selected and removed from the Start menu.

🖰 *Select Notepad from the list below the Programs folder, then click* ▒▒ Remove ▒▒

Notepad has now been removed from the Start menu.

An alternative method of removing items from the Start menu uses the desktop shortcut created earlier in the chapter.

🖰 *Open the Start Menu window from the context menu for* ▒Start▒ *as you did earlier.*

Using this window, items can be removed using the standard methods, such as dragging items to the 🗑 Recycle Bin, or selecting items and pressing delete.

🖰 *Try removing Explorer from the Start menu, using one of these methods.*

Summary: Customising The Start Menu

- New items can be added using Taskbar Properties.
- Adding new menu items using drag & drop adds shortcuts to the Start menu.
- Items on the Start menu can be accessed by number.
- New items and new sub-menus can be added as 'folders' by using the Explorer or My Computer.
- Menu items can be deleted without effecting the program files.
- New installations are added to the Start menu automatically.

INDEX

Networks
  client-server 9
  logging on 8
  mapping a drive 186
  shared resources 8
  workgroups 8, 168
New documents
  creating from desktop 60
Notepad
  introduced 43

O

Object
  hierarchy 119
Objects
  containment 103
  introduced 14, 102
  moving and copying with
    Explorer 132
  object oriented 103
  opening 15
  properties 103
  renaming 124

P

Panes
  in Explorer window 122
Password
  to network resources 8
  to Windows 95 6
Printers
  local 203
  local printers 203
  networked 197
  print jobs 208
  print queue 208

  printer windows 209
  printer wizard 197
  printers folder 196
Properties
  desktop 111
  of objects 103
  read-only 108
  read/write 108
  through control panel 114

Q

Quick View
  Explorer 135

R

Read-only properties 108
Read/write properties 108
Recycle Bin
  introduced 73
Renaming
  documents 64
  objects 124
Resources
  shared on network 8
Restoring files
  See Recycle Bin 161
Root directory 17

S

Safe Mode 4
Save As dialog 79
Scraps 94
Screen Savers 37
Scroll bars 20
Scroll button 21
Shortcuts 140

application 146
  to documents 141
  wizard 147
Sizing a window 19
Start menu
  introduced 40
Starting Windows 95
  safe Mode 4
  startup menu 4
Startup Options 4
Submenus 41
Switching applications 45

T

Taskbar 44
  options 55
Toolbar
  Explorer window 128

U

Undelete
  See Recycle Bin
Undo command 85

W

Welcome screen 10
Windows
  applicationwindows 42
  arrangingwindows 49
  closing 21
  for an object 15
  maximise/minimise 42, 46
  moving and sizing 18
  scrollbars 20
  tile and cascade 52
Windows 3.x 1

Wizard
  printer 197
  shortcut 147
WordPad
  changing font 90
  creating a new file 83
  menu commands 83
  printing files 84
  saving files 79
  the screen 78
Wordpad
  options 87
  toolbar 78
Workgroups 8, 168

Other related titles

T E A C H   Y O U R S E L F

MULTIMEDIA

Multimedia applications bring together the media of text, still and moving pictures, graphics and sound to your desktop PC. *Teach Yourself Multimedia* looks at how this new technology works, how it is being used in business, education and entertainment, and what it will mean for you. The book contains a full glossary of multimedia terms and covers:

- multimedia platforms,
- video playback, sound cards and MIDI,
- multimedia applications,
- education and training.

Neil Fawcett is Personal Computer editor of *Computer Weekly*.

Other related titles

TEACH YOURSELF

EXCEL 5

Teach Yourself computer books provide a full introduction to the major software packages available today.

Teach Yourself Excel 5 is for first-time users of Microsoft Excel for Windows version 5.

The book will give you a complete introduction to Excel. It shows you how to create simple spreadsheets and how to use the spreadsheets for calculations, including writing formulae and using functions. It also covers in detail formatting and printing, producing charts and working with several spreadsheets to produce professional-looking documents and reports.

Once you can produce simple worksheets with confidence, you can also learn how to use more complex features:

- working with multiple windows,
- entering data using AutoFill and AutoSeries,
- setting manual page breaks, margins, headers and footers,
- cutting and pasting across workbooks,
- performing calculations across worksheets.

About the authors
Oxford Computer Training are a leading computer training company. They are twice winners of Microsoft UK's Authorised Training Centre of the Year award for PC Applications.

Other titles in the series
Teach Yourself Word 6
Teach Yourself PowerPoint 4

Other related titles

TEACH YOURSELF

POWERPOINT 4

Teach Yourself computer books provide a full introduction to the major software packages available today.

Teach Yourself PowerPoint 4 is for first-time users of Microsoft PowerPoint for Windows version 4.

The book will give you a complete introduction to PowerPoint, enabling you to produce professional-looking presentations using your computer. It explains the basic principles, shows you how to make effective slides and acetates and how to run a slide show. You also learn how to edit or rearrange your slide show and how to save it.

Once you can produce simple slides with confidence you can also learn how to use more complex features:

- adding graphics to slides,
- using the ClipArt gallery,
- producing speaker notes,
- using PowerPoint with Excel 5 and Word 6,
- producing a fully automatic presentation.

About the authors
Oxford Computer Training are a leading computer training company. They are twice winners of Microsoft UK's Authorised Training Centre of the Year award for PC Applications.

Other titles in the series
Teach Yourself Word 6
Teach Yourself Excel 5

Other related titles

WORD 6

Teach Yourself computer books provide a full introduction to the major software packages available today.

Teach Yourself Word 6 is for first-time users of Microsoft Word for Windows version 6.

The book will give you a complete introduction to Word. It starts with basic word processing and shows you how to create professional-looking letters and documents. You will be shown how to edit text and how to handle documents, as well as how to undo mistakes, how to print your work and how to save it.

Once you can produce simple documents with confidence you can also learn how to use more complex features:

- changing the format of characters and paragraphs,
- creating bulleted and numbered lists,
- creating and manipulating tables,
- checking your spelling,
- creating and using styles.

About the authors
Oxford Computer Training are a leading computer training company. They are twice winners of Microsoft UK's Authorised Training Centre of the Year award for PC Applications.

Other titles in the series
Teach Yourself Excel 5
Teach Yourself PowerPoint 4

FURTHER TITLES FROM
TEACH YOURSELF

0 340 63947 4	EXCEL 5	£6.99	☐
0 340 60902 8	MULTIMEDIA	£5.99	☐
0 340 63945 8	POWERPOINT 4	£6.99	☐
0 340 63944 X	WORD 6	£6.99	☐

All Hodder & Stoughton / Teach Yourself books are available from your local bookshop or can be ordered direct from the publisher. Just tick the titles you want and fill in the form below. Prices and availability subject to change without notice.

To: Hodder & Stoughton Ltd, Cash Sales Department, Bookpoint, 39 Milton Park, Abingdon, OXON OX14 4TD, UK. If you have a credsit card you may order by telephone – 01235 831700.

Please enclose a cheque or postal order made payable to Bookpoint Ltd to the value of the cover price and allow the following for postage and packing:

UK & BFPO: £1.00 for the first book, 50p for the second book and 30p for each additional book ordered up to a maximum charge of £3.00.
OVERSEAS & EIRE: £2.00 for the first book, £1.00 for the second book, and 50p for each additional book.

Name ....

Address ....

....

....

If you would prefer to pay by credit card, please complete:
Please debit my Visa / Access / Diner's Card / American Express (delete as appropriate)
card no:

☐☐☐☐☐☐☐☐☐☐☐☐☐☐☐☐

Signature .... Expiry Date ....